Power and Empowerment
in Higher Education

Contents

Preface

This volume represents an attempt to understand more fully the meaning of power as it relates to higher education. We have also demonstrated a wide variety of forms in which this relationship may be found in American society.

The word "power" stands for the capacity to accomplish positive social ends or to make decisions that influence the behavior of others for the good as we understand it. This "good" or "end" must itself always stand under critical examination, as must the nature of the influence. Plato had, for our purposes, perhaps the most useful understanding of power. He saw the dialectical relationship between the "influencer" and the "influenced." Power for Plato had two dimensions (*Sophist*, 247–48). These were the active and the passive dimensions, or the existence simultaneously of the capacity to influence (active) and the capacity to be influenced (passive). The implications for colleges and universities, as well as for agencies having a bearing on these institutions, are multiple. Clearly the faculties, the administrations, and the students may, under this dialectical conception of power, find themselves in community situations where each can be an agent of power active or power passive or both.

The "empowerment" part of the title refers generally to the facilitating devices and mechanisms employed in various circumstances by which or through which the goods or ends are achieved. Those of us involved in any way in higher education today have not only to take more seriously than ever our professional responsibilities, but we must also work to maintain a constant sensitivity to the great realm of values where "power" and "empowerment" are involved.

While we share a general understanding of the terms employed, there is great variety in the content of the seven papers: there is the problem of maintaining integrity in relationship to educational empowerment in the light of American cultural values and recent national experience (Muelder); the development of the problem of governance in institutions of higher education (Hill); the evolution of the status of the departmental chairman (Clark); the peculiar aspects of the problem of power in departments of religion (Robertson); academic influence in changing political expectations in the United States (Sykes); the Vietnam war and the question of amnesty, showing the capacity of educational institutions to challenge the nation's conscience (Stassen); and the tradition of governmental support for education in the United States compared to other Western nations (An).

This collection of papers is dedicated to Louis Smith, dean and professor of political science and history at Berea College for many years. We trust that this volume may contribute to a better understanding of the many facets of the subject and at the same time call attention to Louis Smith as an educator who knows well the parameters of "power and empowerment in higher education." We regret that one of our contributors, Dr. Norman Hill, died in 1976.

Many people who did not write a paper for this volume nevertheless played important parts in seeing it through from beginning to end. The Committee on Publications at Berea College, of which Dr. Carol Gesner is chairman, initiated and helped to develop the original idea for the book. President Willis Weatherford has given personal encouragement and official College support for the enterprise over the extended period it has taken to complete the work.

D. B. ROBERTSON

Empowerment and the Integrity of Higher Education

WALTER G. MUELDER

To begin with my definitions, integrity in higher education is personal and social devotion to the wholeness of the individual and to truth. It is also responsible freedom dedicated to both social and ultimate values. Empowerment refers to the power education bestows on persons for effective participation in the social, economic, and political orders. I shall try to show how, once education has empowered persons to function effectively, their accommodation to goals of material success creates a tension between integrity and empowerment. The alumni and the larger community share with the faculty and the administrators in this empowerment. They also share in temptations to violate integrity. I believe that the recovery of the humanistic and liberal arts tradition as the nucleus of higher education is required to conserve educational integrity. This recovery is made difficult by the moral and spiritual compromises that have taken place within the liberal arts tradition, even though the formal categories of humanism are employed. The tensions between empowerment and integrity are, accordingly, both internal in the life of the university and external between the university and its environment.

Institutions of higher learning have increasingly been viewed as places where empowerment for participation in the public domain is provided. Strains and stresses of changing political policy and empowerment have challenged the traditional integrity of colleges and universities and have signaled redefinitions of this integrity. Empowerment relates the role of the university in society with its role in culture by conserving values and culture patterns, by criticizing society's norms and methods, by anticipating new modes of society, and in the light of ideal ends by encouraging leadership to move from conservation to innovation. Empowerment in the community is, therefore, not neutral, but embraces the dynamic aspects of the university as a community of memory and hope. Empowerment does not guarantee the integrity of the university.

The use of the university as an instrument of political and economic development depends on the social policy of the university. John Kenneth Galbraith has recently reaffirmed the close relationship of policy and the men and women it specifies for leadership. In turn, the educational quality of persons in positions of leadership specifies the policy that is followed. The relation is symbiotic. Writing for the Pacem in Terris III Convocation and addressing certain issues of foreign policy, Galbraith observed: "While, as commonly imagined, men do have a certain influence on the foreign policy . . . policy has an even more profound effect in selecting the people who guide it." [1] This observation is as valid for higher education as for foreign policy. If, by a process of attrition and adjustment, university policies come to mirror the interests of the empowered, these policies will specify university leaders with the same interests.

The pressures on the university to conform to its social environment increase as economic and political institutions increase their dependence on the university. And these institutions are dependent for the leadership that social policy affirms. The term *multiversity* expresses the plural service roles that higher education plays in the nation. Hardly an activity in contemporary culture does not look to the university for leadership and guidance in proliferating specializations. Likewise, the taxpaying public claims service and usually rewards it. Prestige within the university has drifted with changing times, and higher education has tended to change in response to prestige and pressure. But so long as the canons of academic peace and freedom were observed, the crisis of autonomy and integrity was obscured.

A historical perspective assists in analyzing the problem. Never has the college been entirely independent of its social or cultural setting. Yet humanistic freedom, autonomy, and integrity were its formative ideals. When the liberal arts college and curriculum prevailed as the central institution of higher education, the curriculum may not have been as immediately "relevant" and empowering as it is now. Indeed some historians have pointed out that the small, church-related liberal arts college was not a product of American frontier conditions, but rather was a Christian transplant, a European cultural island in the midst of a pragmatic, rough and ready, rapidly developing sea of real estate, farming, commerce, and industry, where the ministry, law, and medicine were about the only learned professions. The expanding secularization of American life never fully appropriated the liberal arts college and is now in danger of wiping it out in a deluge of vocationalism.

George Herbert Mead noted more than forty years ago: "There is no more striking character of American consciousness than this division between the two great currents of activity, those of politics and business on the one side, and the history, literature, and speculation which should interpret them on the other. . . . This culture appeared then in the curriculums of American schools and colleges. There was no other to put in its place. American native culture accepted the forms and standards of European culture, was frankly imitative. It was confessedly inferior, not different. It was not indigenous. The cultivated American was a tourist even if he never left American shores. When the American felt the inadequacy of philosophy and art native to the Puritan tradition, his revolt took him abroad in spirit if not in person, but he was still at home, for he was an exponent of the only culture the community possessed." [2]

The crisis of integrity in the midst of empowerment today is a crisis not only in the meaning of academic freedom within academe but in the universal relevance of the classical values in the humanist tradition. It is a question of substance as well as of formal integrity.

How did the distortions of humanism come about? There were several sources, but one important development was the marriage of Puritanism, which was the bearer of the liberal arts heritage to American shores, and uncontrolled capitalism. In the formative period of liberal higher education whether in the church-related, nonsectarian private colleges or the rising state universities, the spirit of Puritan Protestantism was a powerful influence. The latter half of the nineteenth century witnessed not only the empowerment of thousands of leaders in the professions but also the rapid development of industrialism. Thus at the time that Protestantism had achieved its greatest dominance in culture, it was making an almost complete ideological and emotional identification with American capitalism. Of course, the roots of this union, as Max Weber and R. H. Tawney have shown, are much earlier. Yet, in the United States, Protestant leaders were the great achievers of the thriving bourgeois society and the free-enterprise system. This identification was reinforced by nationalism and the populist philosophy in politics. So complete has this fusion remained in the American consciousness, that a hundred years later, "anticommunism" is still an almost automatic political and economic response in the world setting. Those liberals who in the "social gospel" movement worked out new patterns of religious, economic, and political thought and action had to contend with a resistance that was all-enveloping. The social gospel challenge may be viewed as part of progressive democratic thought prior to World War I, but liberal theological thought was more often wedded to the capitalist social Darwinism than to Christian socialism. Liberal arts college faculties were seldom strongholds of the left wing of social Christianity even when they affirmed academic freedom against the attacks of the most conservative groups in the community.

Given the further identification by millions of immigrants with the aspirations and way of life of the middle class, and the consequent reinforcement of middle-class behavioral patterns, it was inevitable that the pragmatic concerns for immediate relevance would steadily reshape and redirect the future of universities as servants of high school graduates entering the middle class in search of success. The intellectual center of gravity moved from the arts and sciences to the instrumentalism of most of the professional schools. Liberal arts faculties developed a defensive, even a fortress, mentality against the vocationalism of the professional schools without acknowledging the breaches in the walls of the humanistic stronghold and the consequent professionalism of doctoral programs in many institutions.

This widespread compromise in the interest of economic and political empowerment of millions of young people over a period of several decades must be acknowledged if one is to understand the protests of the sixties and the crises of the seventies. Often the analysis by humanists is quite different, as they interpret the change as something that suddenly appeared about fifteen years ago. This view is essentially intramural. Ronald Berman says: "There have been two revolutionary changes on campus, one material and the other political. From 1958 to 1968 the American university boomed along with the rest of the economy. There were many benefits as intellectual life became part of the knowledge industry. . . . The script for the sixties was perhaps implied by the work of Émile Durkheim, the first modern sociologist and our great theorist of social decay. Students with few connections to their teachers, inhabiting campuses unintelligible without a road map, sitting in classes by the hundreds or thousands, became the natural constituency for unrest." [3] This analysis is true as far as it goes, but the larger fact is that the social policy of higher education had, to use Galbraith's phrase, an "even more profound effect in selecting the people who guide it."

Another essentially intramural viewpoint is that taken by Adam Ulam, writing for the Phi Beta Kappa membership: "Until some fifteen years ago those who ran our education felt no need to question or to apologize for the assumption that the university can best promote democracy and combat inequality by diffusing knowledge, that it advances general welfare by training competent specialists, that it contributes to desirable social change by the very process of enlarging students' horizons and furnishing their minds with information about their country and the world, in other words, by being an institution of learning, by teaching and not indoctrinating, by producing enlightenment and reflection, and not policies or agitation." [4] The weakness of this analysis lies in its barren formalistic categories, for worldly success was easily achieved behind the facades of these categories.

The self-image of higher education on many campuses hardly corresponded to the betrayal of social virtue which it actually served. While holding to the formal categories cited above by Ulam, the faculties designed much of the education with an eye to marketing the product, and to getting ahead themselves in terms of wealth and status. There was widespread pandering to professional and vocational constituencies. One must not overlook the off-campus allegiances of staff and faculty: the grantsmanship, the consultations, the retainers, the divided loyalties, and the virtual apprenticeships of curricula and departments to chemical societies, the performing arts, school systems, advertising agencies, corporation management, professional accrediting institutions, and on and on. Not least important was the symbiosis of university personnel and the military-industrial complex. When recruiters came to the campus, they found many who had gone beyond apprenticeship and were already journeymen. However, when gathered in solemn academic assemblies, faculties and administrators generally indulged in symbols drawn from earlier periods of humanistic rhetoric.

The conduct of universities, particularly public ones, during the thirties, forties, and fifties shows a continual erosion of humanistic and general liberal arts substance both in theory and practice. And this long process set the stage for later revolts and present predicaments. A cleavage of long standing developed between those parts of the university which were essentially utilitarian and instrumentalist in their values and those increasingly defensive parts which claimed to be liberal arts, though they were often seriously compromised from within. One further sign of this internal incoherence and lack of adequate liberal arts philosophy was the awkwardness with which many colleges and universities treated the field of religion. Instead of approaching it with classical intellectual breadth suitable to its inherent ultimate concerns, they often reduced it to literature or history. Whenever a liberal arts faculty deals with a subject matter in a reductionist manner, it displays both its lack of intellectual nerve and its incomplete understanding of cultural values. Failure to address the ultimate values may inhibit addressing the penultimate ethical values needed to preserve true humanism. Ulam believes that "the university became seduced by the great world beyond it" between 1958 and 1960. This seduction was quite obvious then and had chaotic consequences that included disruption, destruction, military confrontation, and even murder, but the seduction is of long standing. It expanded exponentially after World War II.

And yet, no matter what its compromises with history, social environment, or changing social policies, the university became and remains a central reference point for civilization. On a scale never before achieved, the university is the dominant center of organized intellectual life. Youth has idealized the university as the embodiment of what it presented itself as being. Where is youth to turn for intellectual and valuational guidance in the midst of rapid social change, revolution, and worldwide realignments of power if not to the shrines of learning with the canons outlined by Adam Ulam? Because of the obscenities of aggressive militarism, racism, neocolonialism, balance of terror, arrogant nationalism, and urban decay, students naturally looked to the universities for hope and the intellectual basis for an ethical faith. And they found the institutions wanting. "Student extremism" cannot be understood apart from student idealism. The proximate goals of higher education and the proximate needs of students were incongruent; and no higher coherent or humane perspective seemed available within which the rightful autonomy of the student as person-in-community could be conserved. To condemn the students' efforts to politicize universities is to close one's eyes to a context wherein the students newly saw the connections between the extramural and the intramural worlds. The students saw that they had been deluded about the autonomy and integrity of the university, and they charged it with hypocrisy.

We shall consider more fully below certain facets of the adolescent and occasionally criminal behavior of youth, but we shall note a thesis here: at the heart of the university's power to resist inner and outer corruption is the humanistic or liberal arts core of disciplines, ideals, and community of students and faculty.

In the 1970s there is a marked emphasis on "practical studies" at American colleges. Such studies relate to marketable skills and utilitarian values and they tend to downgrade the liberal arts. This shift from general education to vocational education means fewer majors in some of the social sciences like political science and sociology; it means fewer in English, history, religion, and philosophy. Though it is too early to evaluate the situation definitively, it may mean a turning away from student activism and a greater concern to meet living costs in an escalating inflation. A decade ago job offers seemed to be abundant.

Social policy made money available to send men to the moon. Social policy does not now make comparable resources available for men to learn how to live in a world that is a global village with plural histories but a common destiny.

Direction of higher education programs toward specific job openings is one factor in the new vocational emphasis. In such areas as day-care and nursery management, community services and social work, and marketing and quality control, internships seem to have as much a market dimension as an educational one. Increasingly colleges are developing cooperative programs with business concerns. Cooperative education, in which students alternate semesters between campus and a related job, is growing by leaps and bounds across the United States.

This development may be viewed as the product of that long-time trend in which American higher education adjusted and accommodated itself to business America. Those who succeeded in that America reinforced this pattern of accommodation, for it empowered millions to become white-collar and professional workers. Business, politics, and certain new professions, along with the military establishment, have underscored the short-term advantages of this educational pattern. On the other hand, the plight of the nation indicates that this system works badly for those who are not already in the system, those disadvantaged by ghetto backgrounds; and it works badly for the nation as a whole and for the world in the long run. Nevertheless, the vocational trend is continuing.

Some have estimated that by 1980 between 80 and 90 percent of jobs will not actually require a college degree of those performing them, but skills-proficiency will be required. The latter demand will reinforce pressures for more and more junior college-level vocational programs. The proportion of students in liberal arts programs may decline even more, and many small liberal arts colleges may have to close or capitulate utterly in their humanistic endeavors.

This prospect has implications for empowerment in both its economic and its political extensions. Will such a program serve the upward mobility of the disadvantaged? Even in a technological society, limited general education and foundations for skills may short-circuit a satisfying life and effective citizenship.

If, as many predict, the average American will change jobs every seven years in the coming decades because of outmoded technology, the ability to adjust to new situations will require a breadth of liberal arts education and self-development that will preserve mental health, moral stability, creativity, and humane empowerment.

The response to the situation is being felt just when the panic for increasing job relevance is peaking. Some foundations are sensing the dangers to persons and the body politic and are giving assistance to certain colleges in order to strengthen the liberal arts component while avoiding a collision course with vocational education. The American Academy of Arts and Sciences has noted "the increasing awareness of the need for the humanistic contribution to our society and the lack of a proper focus for humanistic activity." The Rockefeller and Mellon foundations are taking sympathetic note of planning activities for establishing a National Humanities Center. Such a center would seek to improve the quality of studies, help generate more substantial support for the humanities, encourage interdisciplinary work, concern itself with current problems to which the humanities can make a contribution, and make proposals to improve institutional bases for the health of the humanities. In these ways the humanistic spirit and point of view would be spread.

Reaffirmation of humanistic values in higher education must take full account of the values that have taken possession of a civilization devoted to science, technology, sensate consumption, and market success. Technology is never valuationally neutral, for it reflects and reinforces certain values in the nexus that produces it. However, many liberal-arts faculty members and scientists still argue that technology is neutral and that everything depends on how it is used. The evidence from the developing countries makes it abundantly clear that there is a conflict between traditional cultural values and mentality, on the one side, and the goals, attitudes, and habits required for technological modernization on the other. Scientific technology is a powerful catalyst of social change in a given direction and requires basic assumptions when applied in either Western or non-Western societies. It is a carrier of the values and ideologies that conceived it and brought it forth. This set of basic values is found whether one is considering atomic bombs and reactors, the military-industrial complex, construction engineering, bureaucracies of business and political administration, systems analysis, Skinnerian control of mental patients, or the biotechnical revolution in medicine. These value assumptions link science with power, detachment with technique, concern for precision with invariability of prediction, empiricism with physicalism, mathematics with reductive analysis, and all these values with the pretense of being value-free. The posture of technology and science in nonhuman areas of inquiry and control pushes the social and behavioral sciences in a reductionist "value-free" direction and puts the behaviorist goal of controlling individuals in the place of a wholistic view of person-in-community. Those who would respond to the vocationalism of technological skills by calling for a rebirth of true humanism must recognize these conflicts of value. Despite the analytical intellectual discipline required for science devoted to technology, its dominant consequence is an anti-intellectualism with respect to the wholistic or synoptic function of reason.

Other value problems are also involved when the technology occurs in or is exported from the Western capitalist world. The application of technology in both business and politics assumes the validity of individualism, that is, of the unit as worthy rather than the community; private wealth and property as the incentive to effort; class distinction as a symbol of success; the middle class as the means of stability; and competition as a method of deciding who should hold power, wealth, and status.

With these assumptions Western society is in deep trouble in today's global village, and non-Western societies are increasingly caught in the dilemmas of the cultural threat of "modernization," Western style. They are also in trouble with technology and development when it is the style of the USSR or of the Chinese "cultural revolution."

Humanists must consider also whether the challenge presented by Ivan Illich applies to the revival of the liberal arts. Illich says that the schools are in crisis and so are the people who attend them. The first crisis is a crisis of schools as political institutions. The crisis of the people is one of political attitudes, a crisis of personal growth. Illich argues that schools have made man distrust true learning and have inhumanly pressed him toward specialization, alienation, and privilege. Will a new humanism seek to overcome alienation by a new empowerment? What form will it take?

The integrity of the liberal arts will require a new integral vision and commitment, one that will address itself to the functional incoherence of American and world society. The revolutionary situation owes less to conspiracies of violence than to functional incoherences of development. Some of these in the political order have concerned a political ethicist like Alan Geyer. He points out that our intellectual and domestic traditions are largely pragmatic and nonideological. And yet, he adds, there is a strong antipolitical bias in the intellectual community and a strong anti-intellectual animus in the political community. To the extent that the religious community has accommodated to bourgeois success-motifs in its institutional ethics, its moral tradition has also been both anti-intellectual and antipolitical. These vectors have conspired to make the diplomatic tradition both messianic and moralistic. The liberal arts tradition is challenged to wrestle with this cluster of problems.

"We do not have," says Geyer, "an integrated humanist perspective on either politics or foreign policy, nor do either our politicians have an integrated humanist perspective on religion. By 'integrated humanist perspective,' I mean to suggest a wholistic outlook in which disparate disciplines and vocations accept one another as natural, necessary, and legitimate partners in the development of personal and social life. In America, however, clergy are anxious and insecure in the company of scholars and politicians. Politicians are embarrassed, uncomfortable, and/or resentful when confronted by clergy on other than ritual occasions; politicians are suspicious of scholars and they are inhospitable and contemptuous toward diplomats. Diplomats regularly curse politicians for obstructing the arts of diplomacy, scorn clergy for their moralism and missionary zeal, and discount the relevance of scholars. Scholars disdain both politicians and clergy. . . . These are false and self-defeating polarities." [5]

One role of higher education is, Geyer writes, "to overcome the partitions of our own Balkanized minds. . . . Ethics and politics must be brought into a kind of federal relationship in which each accepts the legitimacy of the other, there is the fullest possible intercourse between them, and both acknowledge a transcendent humanist faith."

The need for such intercourse has been noted by students. In fact, the student protests of the past decade may be viewed in part as an adumbration of the need for a new integral philosophy of higher education, denouncing hypocrisy on the one hand, and demanding the practice of political responsibility on the other. To be sure, the protests were a complex phenomenon and to understand them we must view them in relation to other such instances, as well as to the various purposes of the political actions taken by the students.

Political action by students has been directed sometimes at public authorities in the name of university freedom and sometimes at the universities in the interest of student power or reform within the university. Sometimes the universities have simply been the convenient place for students to dramatize their abhorrence of political policies and actions, on occasion in ways that are quasi-instructional and quasi-political. Sometimes students have used the universities as a base for ongoing revolutionary action in society in general. Many varieties of protest, noncooperation, or direct intervention (nonviolent and violent) have been employed. Some of these actions have served the university's interests and some have been disruptive of university integrity. Despite their pretensions, students, like faculty and administrators, are frequently the enemies of a true intellectualism, which abhors instant empowerment.

In his definitive study of the politics of nonviolent action, Gene Sharp focuses attention on many different incidents, a number of which have involved student action. In most cases student protest, including the strike, is a temporary action. The student strike is not a new phenomenon, and has been widely used in China, Latin America, even Africa, as well as in Europe and America.

Student protest through strikes in the interest of academic freedom and integrity may be cited from numerous cases included in Sharp's study. When in 1861 it was rumored but not yet announced in Russia that new regulations at the University of Saint Petersburg would virtually eliminate all freedom within the university, students staged an assembly in the courtyard and marched to the home of the curator. In 1935 the students of Bellevue Township High School near St. Louis struck to protest the firing for political reasons of teachers with seniority. In 1940-1941 students at Delft and Leyden in the Netherlands went on strike in protest of the dismissal of Jewish professors. In 1955 at the East German University of Greifswald students struck against a governmental decree transforming the medical faculty into a military school of medicine directed by the "People's Police." In 1960 there was a sit-down strike by pupils of the Fort Jameson Secondary and Grade Schools in what is now Zambia for the purpose of asking that the "political" visits of the Manckton Commission be stopped.

Student action has also sometimes been antiliberal. I have personally witnessed such behavior as a graduate student in Germany during Hitler's rise to power. Reactionary students also have supported various acts to delay or obstruct desegregation in southern universities of the United States.

A common goal of student protest and strikes has been student power and governance within the university. Occasionally there has been joint student-faculty participation. The University of Madrid experienced a strike in 1965 as part of the campaign for an independent student union. Here students attended classes but refused to pay attention. More often, students have used the weapon of school or class boycotts. In addition to strikes for more participation, there have been sit-ins to protest segregated housing and restrictive dormitory regulations. In 1966 at the City College of New York a student sit-in was held in the administration building to demand specific measures for increased student participation in administrative decisions for the college.

Colleges and universities have sometimes been not the object of student protest, but simply the place most convenient to voice political opposition to some national policy or practice not directly connected with the university's own interests or freedom as an academic institution. Following the military invasion of Cambodia by the United States, it became a prominent part of university life to stage protests in the form of disruptive strikes. Some colleges and universities shut down in the interest of safety. Students have tried sit-ins to coerce the administration or faculty to state a public corporate political position on the Indochina war in harmony with the students' sentiments or to change the policies of cooperation with the military or other arm of government. Dramatic disruptions of academic schedules and widespread damage to property were primarily aimed at conscription in general or the draft to fight the Indochina war. In 1943 a student group in Munich published anti-Nazi leaflets, placed them in letter boxes, and then openly distributed them at the university.

Teach-ins were a device to combine educational functions with political action objectives. Persuasion and protest were often combined to promote or to prevent action on controversial issues. Sharp comments: "The teach-in differs from a public protest meeting in that political viewpoints are represented both among the speakers and those attending, and the speakers may be high-level specialists on the subject or otherwise regarded as especially able to provide, not only a capable presentation of their own to the issue, but important factual and background information relevant to the issue." [6] Teach-ins were widespread throughout the United States and England during the sixties.

Political activity has occasionally been used to secure a base in the university for further revolutionary action. During the Revolution of 1905, after the tsarist regime had conceded the reestablishment of immunity rights on the premises of universities and other higher schools, student leaders, in cooperation with liberals and socialists, turned their buildings into political meeting places. Sharp says that as many as ten thousand persons—students, workers, intelligentsia—met in a single evening in the lecture halls, laboratories, and auditoriums of Saint Petersburg and Moscow. Many contemporary illustrations of this kind of activity can be taken from the United States, Korea, Japan, Turkey, France, and other countries.

Efforts at political empowerment sometimes threaten the integrity of the university through inner distortion and create certain dilemmas. Noam Chomsky, himself an activist who has been accused of irresponsible rhetoric, has stated one dilemma frankly: "Those who believe that radical social change is imperative in our society are faced with a dilemma when they consider university reform. They want the university to be a free institution, and they want the individuals in it to use this freedom in a civilized way. They observe that the university— or to be more precise, many of its members—are 'lined up in the service of the war technique' and that it often functions in such a way as to entrench privilege and support repression." [7] The other side of the dilemma is this: "To an overwhelming extent, the features of university life that are rightly offensive to many concerned students result not from trustee control, not from defense contracts, not from administrative decisions, but from the relatively free choices of faculty and students. Hence, the dilemma noted above. 'Restructuring of the university' is unlikely to be effective in eliminating the features of the university that have sparked student criticism."

In retrospect, the behavior of students, faculties, and administrators in the sixties has come under empathetic appraisal and sharp negative criticism. Among the aggressive antagonists is President John R. Silber of Boston University, who charges that there has been a debasement of academic freedom because of the permissiveness of university presidents and the "reluctance of faculties to discipline the liars and frauds in their own ranks." As reported by Philip M. Boffey, the main charge by Silber is that "while the academy had successfully resisted restrictions on academic freedom imposed by outside forces, it had failed to resist corruption from within." [8] "In the actions of these University presidents [Clark Kerr of the University of California, Grayson Kirk of Columbia University, and James A. Perkins of Cornell University], Operation Pander was established and quickly set a pattern for incompetence emulated by administrators across the nation." Among the faculty members whom Silber specifically attacked was Noam Chomsky for indulging in "rhetorical overkill." In the light of this attack the citation above from Professor Chomsky deserves special attention. "The academic," argued Silber, "neither needs nor deserves a greater protection for his political freedom than that afforded the ordinary citizen."

The general perspective and the specific attacks by Silber at the meeting of the American Association for the Advancement of Science were challenged by Professor David Fellman of the University of Wisconsin, a former president of the American Association of University Professors. Fellman rejected the idea that better or smarter presidents might have avoided campus troubles. He observed that the right mix of students and issues would have produced blowups no matter who was in charge. The worldwide phenomenon of student protests, past and present, tends to support Fellman's posture, but, of course, it does not lift crisis tactics of a temporary nature, even at their best, to the level of acceptable policy. Silber's concern for academic autonomy and integrity is commendable, but it must always keep in mind a point well made by Edgar Z. Friedenberg: "Power within the university aligns itself to power outside it." [9] The future of the humanities and of the liberal arts can ill afford to ignore this reality, for freedom within the university is indivisible from freedom outside it. In an open society peace intramurally is indivisible from peace outside.

Economically speaking, higher education is dependent and even parasitic as an institution. Its sources of income are gifts, taxes, and tuition. In a capitalistic society a considerable portion of this income is a levy ultimately on the poor, whether it comes from gifts or taxes. Given the managed market of corporations or cartels, the decisions of utility companies and utility commissions, government grants and controls, the military-industrial complex's financing, or outright taxation, the have-nots carry heavy burdens which the privileged are empowered to lay on them. Through exploitation and the mechanisms of the labor market, commerce, and taxation, the poor heavily subsidize the education of the classes above them. The university cannot free itself from the injustices of its economic environment in every respect, but it ought to have the human insight and moral sense to acknowledge its obligations to all class levels in society—to the poor as well as to the privileged. The empowerment of the poor is not simply an act of benevolence but of justice as well; it is also an act within the indivisibility of freedom and peace.

Equality and excellence are competing values. Higher education, particularly in the public sector, has tried to embrace them both. Indeed, from the beginning of the state university system, the paradoxes and dilemmas of such competing values have been evident. In the context of "free enterprise" and the caste patterns of racism, the justice of equality has conflicted with the structures of privilege. Grievances and alienations were bound to arise. Responses to this situation have varied in different states. In California, a three-tiered system was devised with two-year community colleges on the lowest level, the universities on the highest level, and the state colleges in between. As Gabriel Almond points out, the community colleges were unambiguously egalitarian, the universities were dedicated to excellence, and the state colleges were caught as institutions whose values conflicted, "creating institutional role uncertainty and inviting them into a clamorous upward mobility." [10]

As the student population increased from 200,000 in 1950 to more than a million in 1970 many strains and stresses emerged, five of which bear particularly on the problem before us: first, proliferation of faculty and parafaculty and dilution of institutional loyalty and authority; second, a new division of labor, at the university level, with a privileged senior faculty preoccupied with graduate training and research, a junior faculty burdened with undergraduate teaching, and a parafaculty of teaching and research assistants; third, a substantive cleavage between the sciences and the humanities, with a mood of obsolescence among the humanists; fourth, in time of crisis, a taking back of delegated powers, competition among decision sites, and impairment of authority; and fifth, continuing pressures due to external conflict and crises. Almond observes that in the disturbances of the sixties the activists were recruited disproportionately from the "underprivileged" and "exploited" strata—the nontenured faculty and the teaching and research assistants. He also notes that "the disproportionate recruitment of activists from the humanities departments was determined by feelings of relative deprivation, and a mood of futility and irrelevance." [11]

The humanist and liberal arts tradition in higher education is challenged to show how it can serve well the values both of excellence and of practical relevance in a success-oriented society. The problem is compounded by the fact that as between the humanities and the sciences, for example, the latter have

"a more open relationship to the outside economy and society."
More than 30 percent of science and engineering Ph.D.'s enter
industry and government, while almost all humanities Ph.D.'s
remain in academic life. Morale is further affected by the impatience expressed by the scientific and technological elements
of the university community "with respect to humanist radical-
ism and alienation." [12] This is reinforced by the "antihumanist
inclination and proscience and practical bias characteristic of
American culture and introduced into the terms of reference of
the state universities from their very founding. The values of the
humanities—the disinterested and edificatory study of works of
the intellect and the creative imagination—were viewed as aris-
tocratic concepts to be tolerated and moderately supported at
best." [13]

Perhaps the clue to the recovery of the humanistic and liberal
arts lies in a deeper appreciation for what Talcott Parsons calls
an image of the university as "a community of searchers for
humanly useful truth." The community of the university cannot
reverse the commitments to widespread empowerment of the
people through education and to the role of experts and specialists in society, but it may more clearly espouse the ideal of the
"humane expert." In this quest it will be willing to embrace more
fully the whole concept of "affirmative-action programs," where-
by preference is given to minority groups who have been
pushed out of the mainstream by the inequities of privileged
power.

Given the crisis of American culture and its incoherent urban
civilization, its lack of balanced development, the interdependence of the world as a global village, and the growing dynamism
of the developing countries, perhaps higher education has come
full circle and is now ready to reconsider humane wholeness
and disciplined ways to find coherence amidst the pluralities
of competing life-styles, cultural values, and sociopolitical structures. Within colleges and universities we need leadership that
is both critical of the instrumentalist culture of higher education and constructive in its vision of political empowerment and
of love and reason in persons. In a very profound sense ethics
is still a branch of politics and justice is the harmony of equal
opportunity and excellence. Until fairness is achieved in the

conditions of inevitable competition among persons-in-community, true integrity in the university cannot be achieved. Just because the humanistic and liberal arts are essential and central for integrity in higher education, they must be concerned for the humanist revolution that is the proper goal of political empowerment.

NOTES

1. John Kenneth Galbraith, "The Policy Specifies the Man," *Center Report* 7 (April 1974): 3.

2. G. H. Mead, "The Philosophies of Royce, James, and Dewey in their American Setting," *International Journal of Ethics* 40 (1930): 211–31.

3. Ronald Berman, "An Unquiet Quiet on Campus," *New York Times Magazine*, February 10, 1974, p. 14.

4. Adam F. Ulam, "University and Policy," *Key Reporter* 39, no. 2 (1973–1974): 3, 7.

5. Dr. Alan Geyer is Dag Hammersjkold Professor at Colgate University. The above draws on an unpublished paper, "The Redemption of Prudence: An Ethical Analysis of National Self-Interest."

6. Gene Sharp, *The Politics of Non-Violent Action* (Boston: Porter-Sargent, 1973), p. 169.

7. Noam Chomsky, *For Reasons of State* (New York: Vintage Books, 1970), p. 313.

8. *Chronicle of Higher Education*, March 11, 1974. The observations by President Silber were made at a symposium of the American Association for the Advancement of Science in San Francisco.

9. Edgar Z. Friedenberg, "The University Community in an Open Society," *Daedalus* 99 (Winter 1970): 74.

10. Gabriel Almond, "Public Higher Education in California, 1950–1970," *Bulletin of the American Academy of Arts and Sciences* 27, no. 6 (March 1974).

11. Ibid., p. 9.

12. Ibid., p. 13.

13. Ibid., p. 13.

Democratic and Other Principles
of Empowerment on Campus

NORMAN L. HILL

"Happy the natural college," wrote Emerson, ". . . instituted around every natural teacher; the young men of Athens around Socrates, of Alexandria around Plotinus, of Paris around Abelard. . . . But the moment this is organized, difficulties begin." Organization, he held in his essay "Education," stifles the educational process; it inhibits the enthusiasm that stimulates learning, and it promotes routine: assignments, notebooks, examinations, and grades.

Today's objection to Emerson's "natural college" is that there are now too many students. Committed to mass education, we have no alternative to complex organization. With over 7,000,000 young people intent on an education—or at least on a bachelor's degree—informality gives way to regimentation. Yet, to wrap an institution around education does indeed smother it with "difficulties."

From the beginning the governance of institutions of higher education has been one of those difficulties. To whom should be given the power to make decisions? And what, if any, limitations should be placed upon that power? Candidates for the job of holding power are always plentiful, so plentiful that competition is taken for granted. Some are motivated by personal ambition; others seek power in order to give effect to a program presumed to be beneficial to the students, to the institution, or perhaps to society at large.

This struggle for power, more commonly known as "politics," pervades families, churches, trade unions, corporations, and the nation as a whole, as well as educational institutions. Because its roots lie deep in the unlimited capacity of people to disagree, thinking of it as good or bad becomes irrelevant. It is a fact of life, operative even in dictatorships but more evident in democracies. Our purpose cannot be to eliminate the struggle, but to learn how to carry it on with reason and responsibility.

The campus where the power struggle goes on is a pluralistic society. At one time or another the competing elements have included the board of trustees, the president and other administrators, the faculty, the students, and the alumni. Complicating matters further is the fact that these groups are frequently subdivided into factions. This has been obvious during recent years in the faculty, with conservatives pitted against radicals, and in the student body, with blacks and whites, conservatives and radicals, and even militants. To Clark Kerr this complex resembles the United Nations. "There are," he notes, "several nations of students, of faculty, of alumni, of trustees, and of public groups. Each can declare war on the other; some have the power of veto . . . but altogether they form no single constituency." Representing multiple cultures and torn apart by separate interests, they form a community in which "coexistence is more likely than unity." [1]

Advocates of blueprints for empowerment like to propose reasoned justifications for their plans, especially when basic changes in the status quo are suggested. This was the purpose of the Declaration of Independence, a document which eloquently proclaimed the reasons why the colonies were breaking with England and bent on governing themselves. *The Federalist Papers* were intended to tell the Americans of 1787–1788 why they should support ratification of the new constitution just drafted at Philadelphia. Admittedly the presentations of projects for empowerment in higher education, written and oral, have fallen far short of the inspired language of the Declaration of Independence and the *Federalist Papers;* but in an off-the-cuff way they were designed for much the same purpose. Generally, they advance one or more of three principles of government: legality, which emphasizes the status of the college as a legal corporation; competence, which advocates power where it can be most skillfully used; and democracy (including joint government), which would disperse authority widely in the educational community.

In the eighteenth and nineteenth centuries legal principles dominated empowerment, supporting the authority of the governing boards. In law the college was a corporation operating under a charter granted by the state. As such, the governing board of the college, analogous to the board of directors of an industrial corporation, was authorized to set up needed machinery for the fulfillment of its purposes: a college president (corresponding to the executive head of an industrial corporation), and a faculty (corresponding to the employees of a business firm). In law, the power to run a college was clearly in the governing board.

Before many years this legal justification began to clash with the principle of competence. Critics first challenged the domination of the boards by clergymen, on the ground that they were not equipped to manage the business affairs of the college—the real property, investments, and budget. In response to this criticism, laymen, usually businessmen, were added to the boards, and in time they became dominant. Thus reconstructed, the boards continued their close management of both business and educational affairs.

Later the charge of incompetence was again raised against the trustees, this time on educational rather than business grounds. Businessmen, so the argument went, were having too much to say about educational policies they did not understand. As late as 1918, after the boards had given up much of their authority, Thorstein Veblen of the University of Chicago took to task the boards both of private colleges and of the newer state universities for tampering too much with affairs they knew little about. "Except for the stubborn prejudice to the contrary," he wrote, "the fact should readily be seen that the boards are of no material use in any connection; their sole effectual function being to interfere with the academic management in matters that . . . lie outside their competence." [2]

In 1920 President A. Lawrence Lowell of Harvard University attempted to define the proper role of the boards. He began by pointing out differences between educational and business corporations. In the former, he noted, there are no owners of capital stock as in the latter. The former exist "to preserve and increase knowledge," while the latter seek to make profits. The trustees of the college do not represent private owners, for there are none. He did not, like Veblen, advocate scrapping the trustees but urged that they confine themselves to business. "The scholars," he said, "gathered into faculties, are to provide the expert knowledge; the governing board the financial management, the general coordination, the arbitral determinations, and the general direction of public policy." The relation of trustees and faculty, he reasoned, is "not one of employer and employee, or superior and inferior . . . but one of mutual cooperation for the promotion of the scholar's work." [3]

One of mankind's blessings is the availability of the slow but rather sure processes of practice and custom to evolve answers to tough problems. By the time Lowell wrote, the governing boards in many institutions were already conforming to his standards of conduct and others were falling in line; Veblen's impatience was hardly warranted. Today the trustees are still around, their legal powers largely intact, but modified by an unwritten understanding that interference in educational policy will be confined to exceptional circumstances. In academic matters they have come to recognize the priority of competence and democracy so long as things do not get too far out of line. Their acceptance of present empowerment structures is proof of this change.

Powers of government pried loose from governing boards went first into the hands of college presidents, their deans, and staffs. This was to be expected, for the administrative officials had been prominent among those who had done the prying. The assumption that presidents would be more competent than governing boards to manage academic affairs seemed justified, for they were closer to the classroom. Also, like all executive heads, they were able to make decisions expeditiously. By mid-nineteenth century, the college president was powerful. More and more, as the century wore on, his opponents sought to dethrone him.

His opponents were members of the faculty, who entered the ring to win for themselves a place in government. To justify their claim they at first played up their competence in educational matters, derived, as they believed, from their teaching experience and their specialization in the various disciplines. At about this time the quality of college faculties began to show marked improvement. Instead of the overworked, ill-prepared, and feud-ridden staffs of the past, professors of distinction were appearing on the campus. Able men such as Gilman, Gildersleeve, and Morris, who joined the Johns Hopkins faculty when that university opened in 1876, had attained stature by years of scholarly activity.

The faculty movement had been foreshadowed by such men as the Reverend Jasper Adams, president of Charleston College, who in 1837 advocated that new appointments to the teaching staff be made only with approval of the faculty and that courses of instruction and other matters of academic concern be placed under its control. Some twenty years later Frederick Barnard told the trustees of the University of Mississippi that if it were sound practice to turn the building of a railroad over to a corps of engineers, it would be equally sound to employ experts—the faculty—to manage educational institutions.

By the 1870s presidents of a few of the more progressive colleges were relying heavily on their faculties for assistance in academic affairs. In his autobiography, President Andrew White of Cornell explained that faculty participation there was so effective that he had been able, without detriment to the university, to take leaves of absence for special assignments abroad by Presidents Grant and Hayes, once as minister plenipotentiary to Germany. "The institution," he wrote, "was no longer dependent on one man."

Over the country as a whole, however, changes were slow to come and faculties grew impatient. A literature of protest sprang into being. Professor J. McKeen Cattell of Columbia University wrote in 1913, "The trouble in the case of the university president is that he is not a leader, but a boss," and the word "boss" carried evil connotations in that era, noted as it was for city boss systems like Tammany Hall and the Philadelphia Gas Ring.[4] Professor Cattell thought that recent problems which had arisen at the University of Michigan and Union College had resulted from the exclusion of their faculties from the governing process.

To go into politics, faculties needed power, more than would be implied in the dictum "knowledge is power." They had been slow to discover that in their size and strategic location in the campus community was a latent power sufficient to have a telling effect in an argument: they could shut down the institution if they so pleased. This was a type of leverage that the devoted faculties of a few decades ago would not have considered applying; it was inconsistent with the high, even religious, motives which many of them attached to their calling. Strikes or protests implying a threat to strike did not seem to them or to most outsiders to belong on the campus.

In recent years the mood of the nation and of the campus toward collective action by people united in a common cause has grown more tolerant. High school teachers are unionized and stage strikes despite an indignant opposition here and there. In November 1971, the *New York Times* reported that 133 institutions of higher education recognized collective bargaining and that some 50,000 faculty members were unionized. Even without a union, the faculty of a college, united in its stand, is now hard to rebuff; its potential for troublemaking when displeased has become too obvious to be overlooked.

Democratic principles as a guide to the governance of colleges and universities were first advanced in behalf of faculty empowerment. As the argument went, the faculty was not only the best informed but also the best structured for democracy on the campus. Perhaps this had something to do with its size and the widespread supposition that a large body of men is inherently more democratic as an organ of government than a one-man executive. This point of view harmonizes with the feeling of Americans that their Congress of 535 members has a more democratic quality than their president, though all were chosen by the process of election. In 1887 G. Stanley Hall, president emeritus of Clark University, took note of the trend during preceding decades toward stronger faculty participation in governance (a movement in which he had played a part) and called it a "democratization" of higher education; he expressed a belief that had become widely prevalent.

Another school where faculty participation has been extensive is Oberlin College. The faculty there has been defending its unusual, if not unique, authority in government on the ground that it is democratic. Its nearly complete control of academic policy originated in the "Finney Compact" of 1835, designed to serve as a barrier against excessive interference by the board of trustees in the affairs of the college. In practice it came to be a bulwark of faculty power against the president. The faculty had the final word in the hiring and firing of teachers, in promotions, and in overall policymaking. The president might exert influence, if he had any, but when it came to authority he was a figurehead. The system worked well during the years when faculties and presidents were both dominated by the religious and altruistic aspects of the educational process; when basic motives were alike, conflicts were few and easily resolved. In those early years the president's influence, exerted adroitly, could be equated with power. But the past half-century has changed all this.

Oberlin's last several presidents rebelled against faculty control. They denounced the fact that the president merely presided over a policymaking assembly of the faculty and then carried out its decisions. They contended that they could not reasonably be held responsible for the welfare and success of the college, as in fact they were, without commensurate power. The faculty maintained, on the contrary, that the principle of democracy on the campus was at stake.

The issue came to a head in 1972–1973. A governance commission set up to investigate the question brought in an outside consultant, Harold Hodgkinson. His report recommended that greater power be given to the president. A little later the trustees amended the bylaws to make a few concessions to the president, especially in budgeting and in establishing new programs, but with the stipulation that in these matters the faculty be consulted. By this time the issue had become overshadowed by demands for student power. It remains, however, very much alive.

Waving democracy's banner, students all over the country entered the contest for power in the mid-1960s. For years there had been student organizations on the campuses, often headed by a senate empowered to manage nonacademic activities. Now students demanded a share in academic affairs and freedom from control in their personal conduct. They declared that the curricula and prevalent teaching methods were outdated and that a break with traditions of all kinds was in order. The uprisings of this period require no description; they are fresh in the memories of us all.

Up until this time, latent student power had not been aroused, much less tested. Requests that fell short of outright demands had in many places been granted, with concessions made in such areas as rules of conduct—rules on smoking, drinking, dancing, chapel attendance, or curfew hours for women. But students had seemed unaware of the immensity of the power they could bring into play. And they had appeared reasonably content with their lot in life.

The student power that surfaced in the 1960s, and is still an available resource, is largely negative in character, somewhat like the ability of a faculty to stop the wheels of education by striking. Students discovered that they could demonstrate in crowds on the campus, stage sit-ins in the president's office, parade into a classroom and denounce what a teacher was doing as irrelevant, and burn a building used for military training. Student groups could not only block the processes of education, but with the cooperation of the news media they could publicize their cause in a way so ruinous to a college that its leaders would be scared into capitulation. Whatever the ethical merit of this kind of power may be, its telling effect as a means to an end could not be doubted.

The student movement fused together several sources of discontent: the antiwar faction, frustrated black youth, critics of higher education, and revolutionists. In some colleges when administrators were unsympathetic to their plans for reform, the dissenters created "free universities," the first at Berkeley in 1964, and a year later a second at Stanford; eventually there were some 150 in the country. Operating freely on or near the campus, they set up panels and other informal group discussions of subjects which to them seemed relevant to contemporary living, like yoga, science fiction, women's liberation, drugs, auto repair, election-year politics, and the arts.

While these various forms of protest were going on, an effort was launched by student groups to gain a share in the decision-making processes of the colleges and universities. Their demands were based largely on democratic principles. As Robert Powell, one of their spokesmen, put it, "Student power . . . implies a more democratic standard of governance" in the university.[5] Some argued that the pronouncement of the Declaration of Independence that governments derive "their just powers from the consent of the governed" supported their cause; consistent with this reasoning was a demand that the students be "liberated." A young member of the Alumni Board at Oberlin College wrote of the student movement there, "We pursued two objectives at Oberlin in the '60s—first, to expand the power of students over curricular and extra-curricular decisions; second, to make the college more responsive to social change."

Spokesmen for reforms in government have sometimes used the word "democracy" as embodying the gist of their objectives, but more often other terms which were intended to convey much the same meaning were preferred: "community government," "shared government," "shared responsibility," "joint government," "joint control," or "representative governance." However they labeled the projects they espoused, reformers were clearly advocating principles associated with democracy. This was true in a statement made together in 1966 by the American Association of University Professors, the American Council of Education, and the Association of Governing Boards of Universities and Colleges, expressing a need for "joint planning." Common to the various projects was advocacy of a maximum dispersion of authority to include students, faculty, and administrators. Discussions of policy were to be free and open, and majority decisions were to be put into effect.

Whether the growing support for reform was induced more by the appeal to democratic principles, traditionally revered in this country, than by a healthy respect for the student power that had brought institutions to their knees is not clear. That students were in fact bound by academic legislation in whose making they had had no part could be and was made to appear quite as tyrannical as taxation without representation. Words and phrases can hold power—otherwise advertising and propaganda would be useless. But the power residing in words and phrases mounts tremendously when these are spoken by groups willing to fight for their fulfillment. In any case, the prevalent mood was to give in to the demands. Typical was the recommendation of the directors of the American Association of Colleges in 1968 that "prompt steps be taken to accord to students, as members of the academic community, an appropriate share in the determination of institutional policies with respect to the instructional program and its social framework."

As a result of the power struggle, new regimes of governance have apeared in colleges and universities across the country. They vary somewhat in the extent and manner in which they embody democratic principles and in the compromises they make with the principle of competence. Some regimes are complex; others are relatively simple. Generally they do accomplish a wide dispersal of power so as to enfranchise students. The principle of functional representation used some years ago in a few European nations, under which representation was allocated separately to economic groups, is commonly employed, but adjusted to apply to the three main campus groups—administrators, faculty, and students.

Carleton College is illustrative of the more complex structures of government in which democratic principles have been carried farthest. At the top of the hierarchy is, as in all colleges, the governing board, which in law has ultimate responsibility for the institution. The active center of decision-making is the College Council, composed as follows: seven members elected by the students to represent their different interest groups; seven elected by the faculty with the same stipulation in behalf of internal factions; three trustees; two alumni; and five administrative officials, including the president as chairman. Its decisions, taken by majority vote, are subject to challenge by a majority of the faculty, by a majority of the student senate after an authorizing referendum within the student body, or by the president. In case a challenge is made, the council must reconsider its action; it may then rescind its action, modify it, or reaffirm it by a two-thirds vote. Subordinate to the council are three policy committees: an educational committee, to deal with the academic program (seven faculty, four students, and three administrators); a social committee, to handle extracurricular interests (five students, three faculty, and three administrators); and an administrative committee, to work on budgetary and administrative matters (five administrators, three faculty, and three students).

The government of Berea College is somewhat simpler and gives the student group somewhat less representation. It is more typical of governing structures over the country at large, although diversity among them is pronounced. The students have no spokesman on the Berea board of trustees, as they do in a few colleges and universities; a proposal to so provide was presented and discussed, but affirmative action was not taken. Nor is provision made for a new alumnus to sit on the board, as at Oberlin College.

The administrative committee at Berea, which deals primarily with financial affairs, has no student members; it is made up of the president, three deans, and two other administrative officials. Highest among bodies dealing with academic and campus affairs is a cabinet composed of the president, two deans, four faculty members, and two students (the president and vice-president of the student association). There are thirteen standing committees, most of them containing representatives of the faculty, the administration, and the student body; student members are named by the student association. In addition there are a number of boards and other special agencies such as the student conduct board (two administrators, two faculty, and six students), the rules council (six faculty, six students, and two administrators), and a high court (four faculty, two administrators, and four students). The student association is entitled to name eleven students to attend faculty meetings, with voting privileges.

Prominent state universities have moved in the same direction as the private institutions. At the University of North Carolina, for example, a student government association is represented on all faculty-administrative committees concerned with academic, social, and student-welfare policies.

Minnesota Metropolitan State College is a new state institution designed to serve adult students over the age of twenty-five who for some reason had been college drop-outs, transfers from local junior colleges, and others desiring to work for a degree. After stating that he was not sure that an institution of this kind needed a structure of governance at all, one of the professors, Dr. David Sweet, outlined its components and then commented, "I think we have created an educational anarchy." The principal governing body is the College Assembly, composed of all faculty members and other employees, all students, and all members of a group called the College Association (donors and friends). The assembly meets every three months and is capable of dealing with any matter of concern to the institution. The college has a committee system to supplement the work carried on by the assembly. In defense of the authors of this structure, it must be said that it was designed to operate on an interim basis only, but the time limit for the interim was not stated.

For the most part, alumni have little if any power in on-campus structures. Carleton College, with two alumni on its College Council, is one of the exceptions. It would be a mistake, however, to discount the alumni as a power group. They have enough to offer in the way of influence and financial support to assure themselves of a hearing in institutional affairs. Recognition of this is customarily made by including alumni in varying numbers on the board of trustees; even in state universities where there is a board of regents elected by the people, invariably some alumni are chosen.

An "open budget" is a part of the democratic apparatus of many institutions. The idea is not new, for in state universities taxpayers have always had access to fiscal information; it is novel only in private institutions. Where the open budget is in vogue, the president submits copies of a proposed budget to faculty, students, and perhaps alumni, who are free to criticize and offer changes. This procedure is justified not only on the ground that programs and policies depend partly on financial decisions, but also because it eliminates secrecy, often regarded as an evil in a democracy.

Transferring systems of government from one community, where they have proved themselves, to a totally different kind of community is fraught with hazards. It will be remembered that the corporate form of government, quite satisfactory for commercial firms, was found wanting in educational institutions and had to be drastically modified by practice. Thomas Jefferson, ardent democrat that he was, denied that democracy is adapted to all places, times, conditions, and peoples. "The excellence of every government," he reasoned, "is its adaptation to the state of those who are governed by it."

Communities are of many kinds; they differ in size, nationality, purpose, ideology, and historical background. About the only thing they have in common is people, and people, too, come in many varieties. It has been said that a democracy "is a raft which will never sink, but your feet are always in the water." There would be more comfort in this analogy if we had not seen the raft sink in unprepared Latin American countries. It sank, too, in a Germany unequal to its demands.

Differences between the civil community of the state and the college community imply first of all that inhabitants of the latter, unlike those of the former, cannot lay claim to democratic principles as their inherent right. The right to choose one's government belongs only to a sovereign people. Both in theory and in practice popular sovereignty and democracy developed simultaneously in the western world, and quite obviously each buttressed the other. Clearly the campus is not a sovereign community with ultimate authority over itself. It is a creature of the state, whose right to existence emanates from a charter issued by state officials or from a special statute. In itself it has no inherent right to anything, even its own life. Such democratic processes as prevail on college campuses are there not because anybody has a right to them but because governing boards, acting in behalf of the state, have seen fit to concede them. The motive of the boards in doing so is immaterial, whether they believed their action would promote the cause of education or whether they were intimidated by faculty or student power, or by both.

The transference of democratic methods from the civil society of the state to the college community forces to the front another basic issue: what to do with the principle of equality, regarded widely as democracy's cornerstone. No objection could be raised to the proposition that every student may lay equal claim to whatever personal rights and obligations the bylaws of the institution or the law of the land may provide. The issue here is to what extent, if at all, the rule of equality can or should serve as a guide to empowerment in the campus community.

Within the state, democracy's objective (not always realized) is to enfranchise all citizens equally, with the same rights of voting and holding office. These rights are understood to inhere in the individual rather than in a group. In the college community, however, giving each individual resident the same share in government is quite another matter. As noted before, Minnesota Metropolitan State College is trying to do this in placing administrators, faculty, and students together in a "College Assembly" in which each person has one vote. Composed as the college is, mostly of adult students, this all-out style of campus democracy seems but slightly less venturesome here— even on an interim basis—than it would be elsewhere. The numerical superiority of the students in every college is the obvious obstacle to this practice; the one-man-one-vote principle would place the institution firmly in the hands of the students, with no regard for competence.

If the purpose of an educational institution were to govern, majority control would seem appropriate. But its purpose is to educate, and its government can be justified only insofar as it promotes that purpose. Domination by those who know least about education would be out of place.

By intent the college community is composed of unequally educated persons, with unequal experience in teaching methods, curricula, and graduation requirements. As James Hitchcock and others have pointed out, there is no justification for having professors in the university community except under the assumption that they have superior knowledge and, one hopes, superior wisdom. Ironically the present empowerment of students came at a time when the intellectual quality of the student body in many institutions had been reduced by standards of admission designed to enroll underprivileged young people. If there is justification for offering this kind of an educational opportunity to the ill-prepared, and there may be, then there is equal justification for a diminished rather than an increased student power in decision-making.

It must be remembered, too, that students are four-year members of the community; teachers and administrators will likely be there for many years, some for the remainder of a long career. The input of students in policy will necessarily be based on less familiarity with the institution and perhaps on less dedication to it. This fact too militates not only against the one-man-one-vote rule, but also for a minor student role, if any, in governance.

Establishment of a right to equal or to any participation in college government by students must in some way take account of the fact that they came to the institutions as beneficiaries of many taxpayers and donors, of the distant past as well as the present, to whom they are indebted for the educational opportunity made available to them. In private colleges students pay about one-half of the cost of their education, the remainder coming from endowment income and gifts. In state institutions tuition and fees cover a much smaller fraction.

These limited roles and contributions of students, caused by the fact that they are students and not by any personal delinquencies, explain why their empowerment in institutional government had never been seriously considered until a few years ago. They explain, too, why their present enfranchisement, if justified at all, had to be on a group basis (rather than an individual one-man-one-vote basis) with two other groups—administrators and faculty—also represented. We have set up government by groups, each assigned a fixed number of representatives on the various governing bodies and committees.

The main variant in representation, and therefore in power, is in the number of delegates assigned to the three groups in a given organ of government. Rarely is there equality; inequality to reflect relative interest or competence is the usual practice. On the educational committee at Carleton College, for example, faculty members are dominant, but students dominate the social committee.

In some colleges total student representation in all governing bodies equals, or nearly equals, that of each of the other two groups. Again Carleton College belongs to this category. In most institutions student representation is proportionately less than that of the faculty. This is true of Berea College, where there are in all twenty-one student members on the thirteen standing committees, compared to sixty-seven faculty (some with administrative duties as chairmen of departments) and eighteen full-time administrators.

These hybrid structures, then, pay respect to the democratic principle of equality only casually. Perhaps it would be fair to assert that the three groups on the campus are recognized as equally entitled to empowerment but not as entitled to equal empowerment. Or it could be said that equality is accepted where convenient, but that at many points the need for competence renders it quite inconvenient.

These joint structures, requiring cooperation in a more or less democratic fashion by administrators, faculty, and students, call to mind not only functional representation, as earlier noted, but also international condominiums. Set up during the age of European colonialism by nations competing for the acquisition of the same territory, the condominium was a system of joint government designed to avoid a clash. In 1923 when the city of Tangier, strategically located across from Gibraltar and therefore important to several nations, caused a diplomatic impasse, it was placed under joint control. The legislative assembly contained representatives from ten national groups in the city: the chief administrative officer was French; a Spaniard was the health officer; an Italian headed the justice department; and the rest of the government was parceled out in the same manner. Its virtue was that as a compromise it terminated a dispute. Its faults were these: it was so complicated that natives of Tangier could become dizzy trying to know what was going on and why; it subordinated the welfare of the city to the exigencies of diplomacy; and it made responsibility for failures and successes obscure.

The joint regimes of governance on the campus have similar virtues and faults. They have, at least for the time being, stilled the turmoil and competition for the control of academic institutions. This accomplishment must not be minimized. Whether the mutual distrust of campus groups that was behind the creation of the joint regimes will diminish or increase as faculty, students, and administrators try to cooperate cannot now be predicted.

The joint structures are complicated, too, like the old government in Tangier, and could give participants and observers a bit of vertigo. Guiding a proposal through the maze will require many meetings, delays, and compromises, and much time and patience. Legalistic questions are sure to arise as to the specific limits of the authority of a chairman, a committee, or one of the three participating groups. If cooperation, rather than rivalry, prevails, these difficulties may be overcome.

Some danger exists that, as in Tangier, the desire for harmony among competing groups will outweigh consideration of the well-being of the community itself. It would be self-defeating if college governance (rather than the cause of education) became the chief concern on the campus—if procedures were given precedence over objectives.

Most serious among the faults of joint government may well be, as in Tangier, the obscurity of responsibility for actions taken. Basic to the success of government is placing responsibility when mistakes are made. In a dictatorship the authorship of misgovernment is readily identified, but the people can do nothing about it. Unless a democracy is kept simple in structure, the reverse will be true: there is plenty the people can do about it, but the culprit is hidden in complexity.

With joint government on the campus, if anything goes wrong, the students can blame the faculty, and the faculty the administration, and no one has the time or facilities to find out the problem.

Theoretically every college or university is responsible for what it does or fails to do. A private institution is accountable to the state legislature which created it and to those people who supply it with funds. The public institution is responsible to the state legislature, which, in turn, is responsible to the electorate. Both private and public colleges bear a measure of responsibility to the parents of their students for the kind of education they provide. Most significant of all, perhaps, every institution is responsible to itself, its own conscience and educational ideals; its integrity requires that it perform generously and skillfully its job of providing students with the knowledge and background that will enable them to live successfully. This it cannot do unless it can both understand its function and make important decisions.

The identifying characteristic of a successful democracy is balance. By definition, a dictatorship is an extreme concentration of power; the imbalance cannot be modified without converting the structure into something else. The identity of a democracy, however, is lost when its governing principles are carried to an extreme. This is apparent in the matter of criticism. Without it, the will of the people is neither known nor available as a guide to policy. But when criticism is excessive and undisciplined, it weakens and even destroys policy without rebuilding. Constructive habits of criticism rest on a balance between extremes.

In like manner, democracy requires popular participation in government. Without it, there is no democracy. But excessive participation is equally harmful, driving the government toward ochlocracy, or mob rule. The makers of the American Constitution in 1787 were skeptical of the people's skill in government and might well be accused of having given the people too little power. From that extreme we have swung over to the other: popular election of nearly every official, down to coroner; the initiative and referendum; and mob demonstrations. We call it "participatory democracy." With it is a mystique that "the people can do no wrong."

Distrust of government officials is another point on which democracy demands balance. Distrust is indispensable if the people are to keep a watchful eye on what is going on, and to demand propriety. But if distrust, whether in national or institutional government, goes to an extreme, officials are intimidated, afraid to make decisions, and, worst of all, incapable of leadership.

In educational institutions, as in the nation, there has been a tendency to distrust executive leadership. Undoubtedly college presidents were too strong in the mid-nineteenth century; faculty participation in government was needed, and its accomplishment was healthy. The power assumed by ambitious faculties may or may not have been intended to cripple presidential leadership, but as power was taken from college presidents, so too was the stuff of which leadership is made. A leader needs more than good ideas; with them must go something to bargain with—inducements and the prestige which the possession of authority stimulates. On the campus, as in the nation, occasions arise when decisions cannot await the machinery of legislation or conference. And, like the occupant of the White House, the college president is likely to be blamed for whatever goes wrong, whether or not he had full authority to do what his critics felt to be right.

The leadership capability of college presidents does vary somewhat from campus to campus. But over the country as a whole their predicament is serious enough to have brought forth a substantial literature of protest. Dean Charles Lindahl of California State University, Northridge, charges that faculty power is too dominant and that administrative authority has deteriorated to the point where some administrators are essentially "executive secretaries for faculty committees." In a recent book, *The Degradation of Academic Dogma,* Robert Nisbet advocates a "restoration of the authority of the president of the university, and of the provosts, deans, and department chairmen." John Livingston asserts, "The traditional professorial view of academic democracy, where faculty decides policy . . . leaves no room for administrative leadership." [6]

Surely the expertise of the faculty in academic affairs entitles it to a place, a strong place, in empowerment. Its strength is in its background in education; its weakness is in its processes of decision-making. Its members, wrote Dean Lindahl, are "debaters not decision-makers." In an analysis of a problem, they excel at splitting hairs and elucidating trivia, but action is not their forte. William F. Buckley's statement, however facetious, that he would rather be governed by the first 1,000 names in the Boston telephone directory than by the faculty of Harvard University, evokes a sympathetic response in one who through the years has sat through many dreary faculty meetings and contributed little to their competence. It requires a high-powered executive on a campus to move things along.

From the beginning of higher education in America, empowerment has been a subject of controversy. Surely, the end is not in sight. Professor Bardwell Smith of Carleton College wrote of its new structure, "Anyone who believes that a new pattern of governance resolves all tensions is in for a shock." The struggle for power in educational institutions, the "congenial anarchy," as Professor David Fellman calls it, is too deeply embedded in human nature to vanish.

Never has Emerson's "natural college" seemed less realistic. But never has it been more alluring.

NOTES

1. Clark Kerr, "Policy Concerns for the Future," in Dyckman W. Vermilye, ed., *The Expanded Campus, Current Issues in Higher Education* (San Francisco: Jossey-Bass, 1972), pp. 3–21.

2. Thorstein Veblen, *The Higher Learning in America: A Memorandum on the Conduct of Universities by Business Men* (New York: Huebsch, 1918), p. 66.

3. A. Lawrence Lowell, *At War with Academic Traditions in America* (Cambridge, Mass.: Harvard University Press, 1934), p. 289.

4. J. McKeen Cattell, *University Control, Science and Education,* vol. 3 (New York: Science Press, 1913), p. 32.

5. Robert S. Powell, Jr., "Who Runs the University?" *Saturday Review,* January 10, 1970, p. 56.

6. Charles Lindahl, "Reaffirmation of Administrative Authority," *Liberal Education* 58 (1972):529; Robert Nisbet, *The Degradation of Academic Dogma: The University in America, 1945–1970* (New York: Basic Books, 1971), p. 215; John Livingston, in G. Kerry Smith, ed., *Stress and Campus Response, Current Issues in Higher Education* (San Francisco: Jossey-Bass, 1968), p. 188.

The Academic Hierarchy
and the Department Head

THOMAS D. CLARK

In the vast literature of the history and organization of education, the department head is all but ignored. Only recently, and in light of the threat of organized bargaining, has this academic functionary received much serious attention. It may well be true that the department head as he has existed in the last century of American higher education is an administrative anomaly. His has been a position without clearly specified authority, and the nature of his office in American higher education has had nearly as many variations as there were departments themselves. To a large degree this position is a home-grown one, designed to fill an administrative hiatus between instructional staffs and deans in the actual exercise of academic power.

Behind the rise of the department head or chairman is a long history of the evolution of the university itself. The derivation of academic power in the American university reflects a complexity of historical and sociological facts. Originally most academic power stemmed from the church and its administrative boards of control. Some of it, of course, originated with the family; this was true where colleges became surrogate parents to students. Most of the impetus behind the private or sectarian college movement in America contained a built-in principle which made mandatory a strong control over teaching personnel, curricula, finances, and operation in general. This same sort of control, backed by strong parental urging, acted as an effective extension of paternalism and parental authority into broad institutional areas.

The role of the family, or the patriarchal source of power, was less well defined, it must be said, than were the roles of the church and other supporting agencies. For instance, rules and restrictions imposed as surrogate parental limitations were derived from the whole area of folk customs, social traditions, parochial mores, and, sometimes, literal translations of the Scriptures. Early colleges and academies in America defined their authority in the form of extensive lists of published rules and with on-the-spot, day-to-day disciplinary actions. When a student entered the seventeenth-, eighteenth-, and nineteenth-century institutions he took along with him as part of his human baggage a transfer of disciplinary authority. The president of the college, no matter how weak he may have been academically or personally, was invested with arbitrary authority by boards of trustees and sustaining patrons.

One has only to examine the history of any university or college founded before 1890 to discover how important it was for the president to make a bold show of authority in disciplinary matters. Faculty minutes, annual reports of boards of trustees, and published catalogs supply eloquent testimony of this fact. A twentieth-century student reading these historical documents would have a hard time deciding whether he was reviewing a chapter in the history of education or a report on a public correctional institution. Some of the published rules are within themselves tremendously meaningful documentation of the negativism of early American society.

Many early academic legalisms attempted to reach into the innermost recesses of the human psyche. It is an amazing commentary on youthful temperament that the early institutions of higher learning escaped mass student revolts. It is difficult to reconcile the vaunted rugged frontier independence of the day with the docility of early-nineteenth-century youth. College pranks of the era were almost always adolescent in nature, harmless in execution, and seldom if ever pointed in classic anger against the prevailing power structure. Certainly even the most rebellious student accepted the fact of ultimate authority.

The eighteenth century, and especially its last quarter, may be a revered period, a time when Americans were engaged in defining human rights and liberties, and in establishing these in fundamental and permanent fashion; but it was also a time of tremendous human restraints and repressions in the form of educational controls. The Declaration of Independence, the Constitution of the United States with its appended Bill of Rights, the various state constitutions and their extended lists of human guarantees, and an ever-growing list of court decisions may have established and defined human freedoms within the political context, but these classic documents seem seldom to have been invoked in student-faculty relations in the colleges. No doubt such invocation by an injured student would have branded him a smart aleck, if not a downright incorrigible.

College presidents and professors may have been both loud and eloquent in their proclamations of the objectives of higher education related to freedom, and in their patriotic orations on occasions celebrating the anniversaries of the Republic, or in their lectures before civic gatherings, but in faculty disciplinary sessions they were most often silent on the subject of the application of human rights to the frightened students they held at their mercy in star chamber disciplinary sessions. More often than not they denied the trembling culprits, dragged before them to be tried in quasi-judicial inquisitions, the most primitive access to the most primitive form of consideration of the evidence, nor were the defendants allowed to exercise the means by which evidence was produced.

In the discipline of college youth in the earlier years of academic history there were almost no acceptable bounds as were prescribed for the citizen in the great national ordinances of freedom. Collegiate authority came as near to being absolute as any class authority in American history. It was tempered only by the individual degrees of humanitarian relaxation permitted by the disciplinarians themselves.

Late-twentieth-century rebellion against the mode of application of authoritarian academic power was one of the truly upsetting reversals of academic and social history. This reversal went almost as far in its extremes as did the rule of the older autocrats. Presidents and professors ceased to be prosecutors and trial judges; no longer were they directly involved in student affairs. Their surrogates—deans of men and women, or more recently, deans of students—exercised some of the traditional parental controls.

This area of academic authority had either become so seriously eroded that it could not be reestablished, or authority had been so thoroughly siphoned off by the changes in the behavioral patterns of society itself that it was impossible of maintenance. Within the halls of academe itself there arose special interest groups that sought to establish more liberal civil controls. Whatever changes were made in student-institutional relationships were reflected in professorial-institutional relations. It is a demonstrable fact that professors' rights and academic freedoms became more visible as students gained greater voice in controlling their affairs. University histories again are revealing here. When there have been upheavals among students, their instructors revolted against the established order in about the same degree of effectiveness.

By 1955 the professor himself had undergone radically changed attitudes and sense of his place in the academic hierarchy. Some of his gains were made against the very principles which had awarded him his basic freedoms. The organization of departments historically was a long step toward gaining academic autonomy, and it removed the instructional staff a notch away from direct control by presidents and deans.

Powerful external forces since 1840 have borne upon the progress of American higher education. The vital impact of an intense nationalism began to be felt in the form of inventions, exploitation of natural resources, perfection of machines, and the rise of the city; colleges and universities had to respond. The maturing of the vital energies of the nation created an intellectual ferment which in nearly every way outran the college curriculum.

As the American higher educational system began to respond to a modern technological age, it found itself constantly revising its objectives and its methods of attaining them. Science and research moved more and more into the classroom and often became the central thrust of the curriculum. As American commerce became a central fact both in national life and in the field of international relations, there were more demands for practical, applied education. The pattern of collegiate education, which had been set by the church with the highly restricted objectives of training clergy and teachers and educating the common man to comprehend the Scriptures, now had to give way before an irresistible force. But this surrender was slow in coming.

Across the broad hinterlands of the nation late in the eighteenth and all through the nineteenth century, the college experienced the same pulse of expansion as the state. It not only expanded in numbers of institutions, in enrollment, and in faculty, but it experienced radical changes of form. Inevitably the seminary or academy concept would linger on in varying degrees in all institutions. The "log college" era not only symbolized the influence of the Calvinistic doctrines of the Princetonians; it also represented a break itself with the old puritanical power controls, the classical curriculum, and the influences of sources of support. At the same time, it substituted an authoritarianism of its own. The supplanting of the old strict sectarian control by another which operated from a different social and intellectual base was a mild form of revolution.

Up until the years immediately after the War of 1812, the state had left the battle for the American mind almost entirely to the sectarian groups. The body politic had remained largely silent on the subject of public education, and especially public higher education. The great classical national documents drafted between 1776 and 1787, with the exception of the Ordinances of 1785 and 1787, made no direct mention of the fact that education would be an important element of national life. This was also true of the state constitutions and statutory laws, with only two or three notable exceptions. Even the limited provisions for education in the more recently formulated constitutional documents promised little more than official recognition of the importance of learning. Beyond this was the unspoken hope that some form of applied education would help to lighten the burdens of pioneering and of processing the great store of wealth of the national domain.

Where public colleges were organized, they began as little more than glorified elementary academies serving the classics and adhering faithfully to the ancient trivium and quadrivium of basic education. The rise of state universities such as those of North Carolina, Georgia, Vermont, and Miami of Ohio represented a token break with traditional academic control. The transfer of control from the church to the state was a major step, even though sectarian forces surrendered in the universities named above with the greatest reluctance.

In the years immediately after 1815, and during a bubbling upsurge of nationalism, universal higher education became a more clearly revealed ideal in American life. Two landmark advances in this field marked the years from 1816 to 1825. The first was the inclusion of a clause in the Indiana constitution which provided specifically for a public seminary of higher learning which would be the apex of a public education system. Never before in the United States had this definite association been made of the two levels of learning.

Adoption of the Hoosier constitution was followed in 1820 by the second step of chartering a seminary or college, which opened its doors to students in 1825. This institution was started with the avowed purpose of becoming a "people's seminary," although the title was more promising than were the vague plans for its organization and financial support.

While the lawmakers and citizens of Indiana dallied with the opening of their seminary's doors, a more aggressive step was being taken by a segment of the public leadership in Virginia. The idea of creating a public university as conceived by Thomas Jefferson for the training of intellectual leaders was a truly American innovation, even though it did have a touch of British and continental flavor. The Jeffersonian idea was a highly viable kernel which was to bear ample educational fruit before the end of the century. Whatever may have kept the original concept of the University of Virginia from full realization of its founder's dream, its establishment in 1819 was important. The concept of disciplining and maturing the good minds of American youth for positions of social and political leadership became a part of the national social gospel.

Historically it would be erroneous to assume that Thomas Jefferson's University of Virginia was the first public university; there were public colleges in Georgia, North Carolina, and Ohio. Virginia, however, does have the distinction of being the first institution to make a clean break with the church-bound and minister-dominated academy tradition. Both the Virginia and the Indiana departures meant that ultimately the public state university in America would come to concern itself with curricular challenges that lay well beyond the ancient educational bounds. These would bring departures from Old World forms and traditions both in application and in purpose.

Perhaps the basic concept of the role of higher education in a developing state like Indiana was more earthbound than were the Jeffersonian ideals incorporated in the Virginia charter. Back of the constitutional provision for the Indiana Seminary was the central notion that even in a raw frontier area, the educational process would be stretched out through a considerable number of years. It was conceived to be an indispensable and pragmatic instrument of the common man's progress against a demanding physical frontier. The virtually uninformed backwoods legislators who assembled in the tiny village of Corydon in 1820 were persuaded, some against their will, to establish a public university by the somewhat tenuous argument that the school would in fact become a public service institution. This was true, even though it was more than a half-century before the training of professionals was to begin. Indiana's history was by no means unique. Elsewhere among the growing number of state universities the same evolutionary process was taking place at practically the same slow and uncertain pace.

Faster progress was prevented in large part by academic resistance to change. In 1828 the Yale University faculty prepared what has been known as the *Yale Report,* a rock-ribbed declaration of determination to stand by the liberal arts-classical curriculum. Few documents in American educational history have had a greater national impact on the organization of college and university curricula, or in shaping their central philosophies; in fact every professor who came from the East to the expanding West seems to have brought a copy with him. Certainly the Yale professors had an impact far removed from the confines of New Haven, and this impact was still being felt more than thirty years later. In the western areas of the country where public leadership cried out for more pragmatic education, the classicists turned deaf ears to their cries. No historian can ever estimate how much the efforts to subdue the natural forces of the land, to organize and build systems of transportation that would give national economy the greatest possible flexibility and efficiency, and to train medical specialists were thwarted by the failures of the early educational institutions. Legislators, governors, and even poets (including Ralph Waldo Emerson) spoke eloquently on the side of technological progress. It might be argued with substantial support that the persistence of the old academy concept of higher education helped fasten more firmly upon the American way of life an unrelenting rural agrarianism and an anti-intellectualism.

Legislators and congressmen were often quick to give expression to educational ideals, but they were indeed slow to irritate segments of their constituencies by calling the old-style liberal-arts monopolists into the court of national necessity. It took more than two decades of struggle to bring about the enactment of the Morrill Act of 1862, providing for land-grant colleges and universities. Much of the opposition to this plan of redirection and support of higher education had stemmed from the narrow concepts of what constituted an education in a growing republic.

In general it was not until the passage of the Morrill Act that the American university became a diversified institution, concerning itself actively with the applied and physical sciences. The flourishing universities and the agricultural and mechanical colleges became in fact the realization of Thomas Jefferson's dream of the "people's university" serving the broad spectrum of everyday needs of a democratic society.

Three other events influenced the formulation of the new American public university curriculum with its revised educational procedures and approaches. The impact of Darwinism in the last quarter of the nineteenth century placed major emphasis upon scientific thought and research. This new intellectual stimulus was to have a profound influence on the content of university teaching. As the sciences gained more secure locations in the revised educational programs, the university itself grew in complexity. During this era also came the broadening of the concept of the trained professions and the increased professionalization of subject-matter fields.

American scholars who had been trained in graduate fields abroad, and especially in the later-nineteenth-century German universities, brought back to America new visions of research, teaching, and academic departmentalization. In history, political science, geography, and the physical and biological sciences, the impact of Middle Europe was great. Scholars of Johns Hopkins University were to become enormously important in spreading knowledge about the new university system. The introduction of the elective system after the Civil War was the final blow to the old classical curriculum. This gave impetus to the rise and importance of the academic institution as it has flourished in the twentieth-century American universities.

The present academic department is a child of the closer integration of subject-matter fields, and the broadening of the base of scientific consideration of specialized subject matter. It is perhaps not an original academic administrative device, but it differs sharply from the older European-English mode of the departmentalization of knowledge. The head professorship abroad has been academically distinctive for its intellectual position rather than for its administrative usefulness.

The American department head, and in more recent years, the department chairman, has, historically, served a rather general function in the university power hierarchy. In most cases he has never been an integral part of the central policy- and decision-making administration. His position has grown from an altogether different source, and he has served distinctly different gods. Only when the department head undertook to cross over into the administrative fold did he surrender his prime intellectual reasons for existence. Technically the line between administration and intellectual leadership on the part of the departmental head has never been clearly and universally drawn. A department head in one university might perform a radically different function from that of a colleague in another institution. There might even be major differences in the functions of this office within a single university.

In the earlier American university organization each distinctive field of learning was presided over by a senior professor whose place in the university stemmed from the English and European practice. With rising pressures within expanding institutions, the senior professor evolved into something like an academic administrator. As head professor of his subject-matter field or department, he ideally performed the functions of scholar-teacher; he was also an architect, developing and broadening the considerations of his intellectual interests in the curriculum, and he was a chief consultant in the hiring and supervision of younger scholars and in melding his departmental offerings into the general college program.

In smaller colleges and universities the head professor has presided over broad general areas of cross-disciplinary instruction rather than overseeing a highly integrated scholarly field. Historically this has also been true to an appreciable extent of department heads in many fields in larger universities, and especially in the land-grant colleges which by force of necessity have offered a wide variety of courses in many developing fields. It was not until after World War I that many universities and colleges organized faculties and student bodies of sufficient size to justify much intensive subject-field departmentalization.

In the process of evolution, the power the modern department head has exercised was largely derived from momentary exigencies, his personal responses to his position, his scholarship, and his local campus prestige. As departments grew larger in size and broader in the scope of their offerings, a professional specialist was needed to oversee their operation. This meant delegating to department heads more authority in hiring and firing, in promotions, and in determination of salaries. Where these powers were rather generously delegated by the central administration, the departmental administration became a highly autonomous academic operation.

Obviously the great majority of department heads in most universities and colleges never exercised fully such autonomous power. Rather they had only the most tenuous control over both staff and departmental functions. Often the head's position has been little more than that of an educated, white-collar errand boy. This has been especially true where strong-willed deans have exercised or abused the full power of their offices.

A strong academic personality with good scholarly qualifications at the head of a department has often been able to become a positive power within a university. In addition to overseeing an internal departmental program, he has often been able to become a powerful figure in general institutional planning. By gathering about him a group of productive scholars, the imaginative head has always been in a position to nudge university administrations into providing library, laboratory, and housing facilities sufficient to permit scholarly growth and maturity.

There was perhaps not a single important department of scientific study in America before 1930 which did not have a history of having had at its head a strong aggressive scholar; many such men became the honored veterans and stars of university histories. The same thing can be said for departments which have built outstanding library collections, developed notable specialized curricula, founded university presses and publication outlets, and built good national reputations. Behind a great body of American university progress has been the force of aggressive department heads. It would not be at all farfetched to say that the images of universities up to 1945 have reflected almost as much the quality of the heads of departments as they have the accomplishments of their deans and presidents. By the same token, failure of universities to grow intellectually has often been attributable to the failure of subject-matter departments to aspire to academic maturity.

It is necessary to emphasize repeatedly the fact that no general description can be made to fit all academic departments. No two heads of departments, or departments, for that matter, have been historically alike. Ironically, with all the educational planning that has gone on in American institutions of higher learning, and with the massive literature such planning has produced, the position of department head, even as the department itself, has been inadequately defined. Thus it has been only natural that there has prevailed from time immemorial a vagueness about the headship. In earlier years, more often than not, departments were called upon to perform a multiplicity of duties not strictly within the domain of a given subject. In such cases the head professors acted more as supervisors of service areas than as specialized scholars devoting attention to a learned discipline. Conversely, a given field within itself might have been divided among several specialties. Thus departmental administration has been fragmented by the self-interest of professors within broad fields of learning.

The greatest variations in the nature of heads of departments have often been revealed in the exercise of power. Some institutions, especially the larger and more diversified ones, have de-

manded that presidents and deans give so much attention to
the public areas of their administration that too little time has
been reserved for internal operations. In such instances departments have assumed or asserted a more generous amount of
autonomy, often declaring themselves off limits to meddling by
presidents and other central administrators. Usually such institutions have had frequent traumatic moments of reorganization
and realignment. No statistician could produce a satisfactory
chart showing the amount of time faculties have spent in making
self-studies of their colleges and universities; nor could one cal-
culate the high proportion of time and concern expended on
fundamentally departmental matters. One might have even more
difficulty measuring the effective returns from the expenditure
of so much energy.

Some major universities have no doubt suffered serious damage at times to their internal programs because of sensitivities
aroused over the exercise of departmental and college autonomy.
No better example could be cited than the development of
graduate schools out of the ribs of departments, which have
often been very reluctant to surrender any portion of their autonomy—sometimes, even in such areas as admissions, degree
standards, and the placement of graduates.

Perhaps less damage has actually resulted from strong, aggressive, and autonomous departments than from those that had
nominal heads, but were actually administered from above by
autocratic deans and presidents. Seldom if ever has the history
of departments of this sort reflected much scholarly productivity
or innovative teaching. Heads or chairmen who have functioned
under these conditions have seldom risen professionally above
the workaday level of seeing that minimal teaching schedules
were fulfilled and that the formalities prescribed by institutional
administrative hierarchy were observed. In the happiest of
departments of this latter category the department head has been
almost always a head professor. Occasionally one of the old-style
head professors truly distinguished himself and his institution
both at home and abroad because of his competence as scholar
and professor, gathering about himself a small coterie of equally
competent colleagues. The system, however, was generally so
geared as to frustrate such favorable results, and department

heads have become technical nonentities in the overall exercise of institutional power.

Perhaps the most dependable gauge of the strength of a department head under the earlier organization of universities was his relationship with deans, both undergraduate and graduate. Almost always the line of authority in these areas has been so finely drawn that it has been difficult of definition, but to permit its being crossed could be injurious. The deans, however, have operated from much more clearly defined positions of authority and ultimate power. They have been able to exercise powers over departmental decisions which have been of the utmost significance: they have had authority to approve or disapprove appointments and promotions, as well as salary amounts. Deans as personalities have, of course, varied as much as have department chairmen, but deans, in their well-defined positions, have had more readily available to them the basic controls and the authority to apply most of them. Because of this it has been a generally established fact in the history of university administration that the more aggressive department head not infrequently found himself in a contest with his dean. Historically the weak head either submitted willingly to the dean's domination or even invited, by his own sycophantic behavior, departmental invasion. Few deans of American universities, no matter how erudite, have been sufficiently well grounded or have had broad enough experiences to deal effectively with a wide diversity of subject-matter fields in attempts at departmental direction from their offices.

For at least a century in the immediate past history of our national educational experience, objectives and characteristics of colleges and universities have varied widely. Some schools have been highly responsive to religious doctrinal pressures, while others have responded to special social and political interests. A fairly large number have been contantly aware of political influences and public sensitivities, although the more established institutions have largely risen above them so far as day-to-day operation has been concerned.

Inevitably these tremendous institutional variations have shaped departmental policies. Some departments have had to choose between exercising extremely narrow intellectual controls over instructional programs and facing constant intimidation by threats of withdrawal of support from organized religious and political interests. The state university has ever been aware of the possible damage of public criticism. No better example of attempted public interference with intellectual freedom can be cited than the great furor in the 1920s about the teaching of evolution in public colleges and universities in the South. Even in states where the freedom of teaching and investigation were not actually interdicted by legislative action, there was an over-developed timidity about tempting the wrath of a part of the public. In the late 1940s and early 1950s the McCarthy threat and the supercharged efforts of various veterans' patriotic organizations had deleterious impacts on academic freedom. Thunder from these distant storms was enough to disturb many administrations.

No American state-supported institution has ever been allowed to forget the many faces looking over its shoulder—faces of voters, legislators, and governors, to say nothing of those representing corporate interests. Budget-making time has always meant freshening memories of the lurking threats that can be stirred into action over the slightest public reaction to a controversial issue. Private institutions have been no less responsive to their supporting constituencies. A significant number of academic upheavals have thrust department heads into the front lines of defense of freedom, even when they themselves might have enjoyed lynching the instigator. On the other hand some heads have been forced to retreat at the first rumble of controversy. Academic annals contain the accounts of true heroes who have driven the wolves of bigotry back from the fold of academic freedom. The enemy without has at times included presidents of colleges, deans, governors, legislators, angry citizens, patriotic societies, and religious groups. In the same pages of academic history many a weak-kneed head of a department stands nakedly revealed as a coward who failed in the face of attack.

Historically the department head may have been greatly favored by the rapid growth and expansion of institutions of higher learning. Since 1880 he had opened to him two main channels of advancement. Many a head planned and nurtured strong teaching programs which produced fine scholars, and these in turn raised higher the swells of revolution in fields of advanced learning. Ever beckoning also was the field of scholarly research and the encouragement of original scholarship. Significantly, a good percentage of heads responded to these challenges.

Unlike presidents and many deans, the department head has never been expected to abandon scholarship for life. Like his departmental colleagues he has been called upon to be teacher and productive scholar, exercising his administrative responsibility between times. No member of a university staff stood more in danger of damaging comparison than the head of a department; this was the position's particular kind of emotional cross to be borne.

There is scarcely a history of a contemporary university which does not single out a group of respected department heads who distinguished themselves more as scholars than administrators. In fact, in the final analysis administrative achievement is almost always overlooked. Not only have the stalwarts at times been cast in roles of defenders of freedom of teaching and investigation—they themselves have been pioneers broadening the frontiers of new knowledge. Doubtless the really fine departmental leader never performed a more virtuous act than effecting and maintaining conditions conducive to creative scholarship on the part of his colleagues, or setting sincere examples of intellectual concern and diligence.

Times have indeed changed. This essay has been cast in the context of the past. Perhaps colleges and universities have progressed; certainly departmental procedures and management have undergone fundamental changes. As new and more openly aggressive generations of professors have joined university staffs, they have brought with them different dedications from those of their predecessors. Many of them have been oriented more toward specialized teaching and research assignments than toward departmental and institutional loyalties. The day has passed when a professor could step into the breach of departmental emergency and teach almost any course in the schedule. Newer generations have looked upon the older type of departmental head with decided suspicion, imagining that he was a powerful threat to their intellectual and professional advancement. They may even have come to view him as a barrier to the liberalization of departmental curricula—or to promotions, tenure, and all the other necessary achievements which fill dearly cherished curricula vitae. They have been more demanding of all kinds of rights and privileges, and they have been successful in their demands. In much of the past three decades—especially until the mid-sixties—academic jobs have been available almost for the asking; the new staff member has often come into a department at a much higher rank than his older colleagues enjoyed at his stage of development, and the new scholar has often extracted hiring commitments giving him a fairly secure position from the outset.

With the passing decades have come policy, consulting, and reviewing committees which have gone far to preempt almost all of the authority earlier department heads ever exercised. In many instances, particularly in larger institutions, department meetings have been turned into impersonal and factional bodies haggling over parliamentary rules of order. At no time do they generally reveal more lack of decision than in the employment of new staff members. It is not unusual for a recruiting committee to spend an enormous amount of precious time in a conscientious search for the best possible candidate for a job only to have its recommendation overruled by a single ill-advised parliamentary maneuver.

A fundamental weakness, historically, in the department headship was the ease with which it could be overturned by the administration or by staff reactions. The position of head was almost always without tenure and without specified term. The head has likewise always been administratively a middleman. But the modern rotating chairman has become to a shameful degree a master of paperwork and a liaison officer between staff and administration. He has had little more voice than the lowest-ranking voting member of the department. Again the variations in chairmanships are as numerous as ever, but the present variations are largely in kind and not in the status of the position. The onerous duties of the chairmanship have tended to drive earnest scholars away from the position. It is a rare modern chairman who can attend to the endless administrative details of a large academic department and at the same time make any pretense of teaching and carrying on research. Likewise, the position of department chairman is not an especially good stepping-stone to higher administrative preferment as the old-style headship might occasionally have been.

With the rise of collective bargaining in American universities, the department chairmanship promises to be thrust even deeper into the bog of anomaly. If unionization gains a firmer foothold on the campus, it is not at all unreasonable to think that so unacademic a body as the National Labor Relations Board will undertake the classic problem of determining precisely what powers the chairman does exercise. A central question for the federal bureaucratic officials will be whether or not the chairman is a supervisory functionary in the sense of an industrial plant foreman or only an intermediate figure in the traditional university administrative organization.

On a broader front, both the nature of the chairman's job and its historical position have lost meaning in many universities. Yet in the passing of the old-style headship some grateful soul should take time to engrave on its tomb a eulogistic note of appreciation for the fact that many a forceful and productive head helped to create a much stronger and more imaginative system of American higher education.

Notes on Departments of Religion

D. B. ROBERTSON

There is a fairly long tradition of interest on the part of philosophers, theologians, and sociologists in the relationship between religion and power. We think, for example, of such men as Karl Marx, Max Weber, Walter Rauschenbusch, Paul Tillich, Reinhold Niebuhr, Martin Luther King, Jr., and such studies as those of Paul M. Harrison. While Ronald H. Bohr complained some years ago about the dearth of "scientific" studies of religion and power, other types of studies are available.[1] Since the 1960s, particularly, institutions of higher education have been studied more intensely than ever as maelstroms of conflict and power, but the studies generally have dealt with the total institution or with aspects of the whole; studies of particular departments within colleges and universities have rarely attracted serious students of power and empowerment. It is probably correct to assert that there has been no published study of departments of religion as centers of conflict and power; yet departments of religion have unique characteristics which make them fit subjects for such studies. The point will be elaborated in a number of ways.

But first, how shall we understand the nature and content of higher education in order to see the place of religion within it? James Luther Adams gives us a definition of his own and reminds us of one offered by Robert L. Calhoun. "In general, higher education is that social discipline which aims to provide those skills of a non-vocational or non-professional order which are necessary for critical intellectual activity and for effective communication between the members of society; it aims also to provide that knowledge which will supply an adequate perspective for meaningful participation in those cultural activities

that go under the name of 'civilization'; and, finally, it aims to
elicit that moral integrity which is indispensable for responsible,
noble living. More succinct is the definition offered by Professor
Robert L. Calhoun, when he says that the marks of higher
education are 'trained intelligence, free inquiry, a critical temper,
and responsible adherence to a clear-headed world outlook.' " [2]
The first parts of these definitions place us, as professors, under
the broad apron of responsibility in higher education, but the
concluding words move toward another dimension.

Both "responsible, noble living" and "responsible adherence
to a clear-headed world outlook" are goals shared with all
academicians; nevertheless these words take on a deeper significance for departments of religion. The words suggest, first of
all, humanistic values. They also suggest a dimension that tran-
scends particular time, place, and circumstance. The point can
be elaborated first by indicating particular dimensions of the
department as "power center," and second by taking account
of our prophetic inheritance marked off strikingly by Karl Marx
and extended by Reinhold Niebuhr.

A religion department is a "power center" in that it has the
capacity to affect the lives of others and to make decisions that
achieve desirable social ends. Further, a department is invariably
involved with a tradition that lays claim to a final truth, a claim
to be considered later.

First, a department of religion has funds to dispense for
programs, colloquia, and special events, and for salaries for a
staff of professors, secretaries, assistants, and visiting professors.
A variety of implications lie here. "Funds" constitute economic
power. While no one in a given department—not even the
chairman—exercises total control over this power, little insight
is needed to see that funds can be used for more or less creative
or imaginative programs, and that they can be disbursed in
keeping with more or less justice among the various members
of the department, or various groups within the student body.

Moreover, a department of religion competes with other departments for operating funds, for students, and for prestige and
influence in the college or university as a whole. This suggests,
among other things, questions about the degree of sensitivity
and concern in religion departments about the programs and

needs of colleagues in other departments. Where does active development of a good departmental program tend to become unfair competition? Where does "healthy competition" with other departments turn into vanity and pride which lead to growth that has lost sight of ends? Academic departments are not noted for self-sacrifice. However, departments of religion may be expected to have retained some capacity for distributive justice. One department chairman writes that he has resisted pressure within his department to push for the hiring of a sociologist of religion. The reason he gave for his resistance was that he knew that one or two other departments were more in need of help, and that his department of religion had special funds unique to the department—for visiting professors, special programs, and the like.

Competing for students is certainly not in itself questionable practice. It is in the form the competition takes where proper questions may be raised. To use an extreme example, surely no respectable professor of religion would be caught peddling a form of the "gospel" sometimes used by Protestant preachers: "We have a bill of goods to sell!" Yet even course titles and advertising of courses can constitute a questionable exercise of academic freedom—translated "academic power."

A department of religion has the power to develop a program of study, graduate and undergraduate, with its distinctive and decisive marks of concentration and emphasis. Professors of religion probably do not sufficiently appreciate the degree of freedom generally enjoyed to develop their curricular offerings without effective interference from anyone. The limitations are usually defined by the competencies and interests of the faculty members. An obvious corollary to such grand freedom is a weighty burden of responsibility; for this freedom constitutes a vast power over students and over the views and opinions of "religion" they transmit to society.

A given department of religion may be distinguished by a number of factors. Certainly the curriculum reflects the overweening interests and values of a department. A "good curriculum" may be expected to offer students rich selections of courses, neither too diverse nor too narrow in terms of subject-matter coverage. It may be fair to ask if a department should have absolute freedom in the curricular question. Colleges and universities do have, of course, curriculum committees, but these committees hardly deal substantially with a department's over-all configuration of course offerings. In case, for example, a department should neglect an important area of concern in religion, should there be some sort of regular appraisal commission, or visiting committee, made up of persons both inside and outside the university—something like Lehigh University recently established? Student participation on such a commission should not be neglected. We are not concerned here with university-wide governance (that has its own peculiar status) but only with curricula of departments of religion. Undergraduate and graduate students could be democratically chosen as members of an appraisal commission. Such a development could result in less resentment against the untouchable power of the faculty and possibly provide the experience of the responsibilities of power. Such an arrangement may enable the faculty and administration of the department to exhibit their capacity to exercise Plato's "passive power," that is, the capacity to be influenced rather than the capacity alone to exercise influence. The display of such passive power could constitute a dispersion of power—the dispersion of passive power and active power among faculty, students, and other members of an appraisal commission.[3]

A special note about graduate programs in departments of religion is necessary. We can assume that graduate programs, like all serious programs in education, have as their purpose service to the institution in its growth and development, service to the student body, and service ultimately to society. Consistent with the thesis of this paper is also a service, variously conceived, to "religion" itself.

What group of planners, however, could deny that a prime consideration in the development of graduate programs is departmental prestige, both within the university and in the confraternity of religion departments nationally and even internationally? Graduate programs also provide faculty members with built-in engines for pursuing their private research and writing. Again, it may be fair to ask whether undergraduate courses tend to become lower-level reflections of graduate faculty interests and seminars—with diminished consideration for undergraduate needs and interests.

A related point is that some of the important questions about power relations in departments of religion have been stimulated in recent years by the development of the office of "director of graduate studies" or its equivalent. The purpose of this office is clearly to aid in the organization and administration of first-rate graduate programs. The result has no doubt been better graduate programs in religion. Beyond responsibility for the graduate program the "director of graduate studies" tends to become a sort of associate chairman of the department in all areas of departmental affairs. This may merely be a matter of good organizational structure and of efficient division of labor. It may be a working acknowledgment that no aspect of departmental life is unrelated to the graduate program—but neither is any aspect unrelated to the undergraduate program. In spite of earnest denials, are not disproportionate amounts of attention and departmental resources given to the graduate program? The importance of first-rate graduate training is not the issue; it must be assumed that much time and concerted attention should be given to it. But the number of graduate students is minuscule compared to the number of undergraduate students enrolled. Even religion majors often outnumber the graduate students by substantial factors. Would not the total program of the department be more reasonably balanced and clearly demonstrated if a parallel office of "director of undergraduate studies" were established?

Departments of religion are agencies of influence—both individual and social. As bland and limited as this influence may be, it is nevertheless an exercise of power, and the consequences may be great. It could be argued that the claims of any considerable degree of influence over students who study with members of departments of religion is false or clearly presumptuous. The claim may be exaggerated, but certain factors are to be considered.

There is probably always a degree of intent to influence, even persuade, students to follow our "line." Where there is a conscious effort not to influence students, our biases play tricks on us anyway; our presuppositions usually peek through our

academic gowns. There is, in any case, the opportunity to exercise influence over students. Where opportunity exists, special
care must be taken.

It is clear that professors of religion often do in fact develop a "following," and they usually do not resist such a development. This may not lead to as strong and lasting attachments
for undergraduates as for graduate students, but it does happen
even here. Graduate students almost inevitably become "disciples" of some person or some line of thought, and they carry
this loyalty with them into their professional work—which is
usually teaching. They, in turn, pass on the message to their
students, at least for some time; and even if they eventually
develop an independent position of their own, they hardly ever
erase the mark of the mentor. And, they, in turn, become another link in the deterministic chain.

The power exercised by a professor in this way may be considered harmless, or possibly even creative. Why not? But is it
possible to be engaged in "no-fault" teaching? Responsibility for
religious influence (or influence over people's thinking and practice of religion) is more serious than other kinds of influence
because of religion's relationship to the ultimate.

Departments of religion control to a great extent the religious competence or incompetence of the students they train
for society. It has been suggested earlier that higher education
"aims to provide the skills of a non-vocational or non-professional
order." [4] This should probably still hold, particularly for undergraduates in religion. There are members of religion faculties,
however, who grandly proclaim that even for graduate students
future employment is a question totally apart from the current
educational enterprise in religion. Yet often the same persons
who assume this heroic posture are the first to boast to colleagues in other universities when "our" people find positions.
Placement records in addition can affect graduate school advertising for potential students for a given program. In any
case, even if departments of religion keep pretending that they
are not interested in the vocational aspect of "the field," we
shall nevertheless continue to train people to teach religion at
a time when the possibilities for employment are diminishing.

It is a disservice to students and to the society which needs the benefit of their training and creativity in other areas.

Perhaps departments of religion will have to consider changing much of their emphasis, and this may possibly mean more stress on the training of such church functionaries as ministers and religious education directors. Some graduate departments are warning incoming students that the job situation is bad— that nothing can be promised when the M.A. or Ph.D. is completed. Some schools are admitting fewer students for advanced degree programs. In any case, the employment problem is not an incidental one. One possibility would be for religion students to go the way of art students and many music students, who are not conditioned to anticipate conventional academic employment. Just what new and unconventional forms employment for religion Ph.D.'s may take is a topic for imaginative study and effort. Some signs of interest in this question have appeared in a few institutions of higher learning. It is still a fair question to ask whether departments of religion should be at all interested in returning to some form of service to religious institutions in their programs.

It would hardly be alien to suggest that departments of religion call to mind the church, which once upon a time (if it does not still do so) contributed to their existence. Departments of religion are sometimes conspicuously high-handed in their manner when they declare to the churches what theology is and is not and yet scorn the institution they would instruct. They need not be so high and mighty about performing some service for the churches beyond the needed intellectual disciplines and theological speculations. Why not explore, for example, new forms of leadership suited to a "world turned upside down"? Such considerations need not fall into religious functionalism.

We are led, now, into a more basic consideration. What are the most extreme and problematical claims of religion? These most tantalizing words were written by Karl Marx in 1844: "The criticism of religion is the premise of all criticism." Marx saw in religion, as he says in the same work, "the opium of the people," an agent that provided a powerful sanction for injustice and exploitation. The claim of religion is obviously more comprehensive than socioeconomic realities. In Reinhold Niebuhr's words, "In religion we have the final claim to absolute truth." [5] All functionalist theories of religion fall into the Marxist error.

This "final claim to absolute truth," in spite of the influences of science, of secularism, of the "death of God," is still a bone in the throat of departments of religion, as well as of other agencies of the "final claim." Academic religionists may attempt to flee it like the wrath to come, but in spite of our deliberate one-step removal from church and chapel, the religious claim simply will not go away. For all our appropriately critical stance as academicians, our devotion to "truth" and objectivity, the reality of the absolute claim clings like a damp garment. Even in our denials we pay tribute to it.

There are two related phenomena briefly to note: first, the large percentage of the faculty of departments of religion which maintains ordination in some church and generally tries to stay in good standing with a denomination; and second, the apparently high representation of members of departments of religion in academic administrative positions.

The first phenomenon is no doubt related to the educational route to the academic teaching of religion predominating into our own day. Until recently the route was usually that of college, seminary, and a university Ph.D. degree, or less frequently a seminary Th.D. One is tempted to speculate about what differences may be expected from the developing route into academia today: the undergraduate degree to the university M.A. and Ph.D., or directly from college to the university Ph.D. Perhaps immediate pertinence lies in considering how, if at all, ordination influences teachers of religion in colleges and universities. The subject is not a simple one, but we are not without some trustworthy evidence on the question.

In 1970 Thomas W. Ramsbey completed a doctoral dissertation at Boston University entitled "The Ordained Protestant Professor: An Empirical Study of Role Articulation." Some of Ramsbey's general conclusions would appear to support the thesis that most members of departments of religion do not escape the "taint" of their religious-cultural heritage.

The ordained Protestant professor for the most part complies "with a sufficient number of the expectations for the role of clergyman to be clearly identifiable as occupying that position along with the position of professor." These clergy functions were found to be performed either on the campus or off, and sometimes both. The most obvious example is the professor-clergyman who acts informally as pastor-counselor, not only to students but often also to members of the college or university staff. To a significant degree, but not so frequently, the professor-clergymen were found to be active as part-time pastors to churches, performing the usual liturgical, preaching, and administrative roles.[6]

There is a fairly widespread impression that a disproportionate number of religion professors find their way into administrative positions in colleges and universities. No empirical data have become available to prove or disprove this impression. If the impression bears any degree of validity, there may be multiple explanations for it.

Most religion professors have had some organizational experience in churches or community affairs, and this may fit them well for academic administration. These professors have often been involved in reconciling serious differences and conflicts between groups and individual persons. They usually have a broad, humanistic background that allows them to move beyond the perspectives of narrow specialization. On the other hand, experience in even part-time pastoral work has given religion professors the practical exercise of power and authority. They have been the mouthpieces of the "absolute claim to truth." There may possibly reside in the minister-professor a fair measure of the will to power that is related directly to the experience of being the "wearer of the gown." The exercise of power is no less sweet when exercised by "the religious." It just may be a mite sweeter.

University "A" and University "B"

Another approach to the basic questions and issues posed here is to take two university departments of religion that represent two different approaches to the use of powers in educational institutions. Obviously no one department in existence reaches the extremes suggested for either model; some aspects of these models will, it is hoped, be suggestive for most departments, whether in colleges or universities. Many aspects apply more directly to universities than to colleges where no graduate program is present.

University "A" may out-Marx Marx in its emphasis upon the function of thought as an instrument of social change. Education as a whole becomes the instrument. The orientation may not, of course, be ideologically Marxist-inspired at all. A fair part of the preoccupation is possibly a version of "the American way," or the compulsion to "be practical." But University "A" as a type or model did no doubt gain status and momentum from the student strikes and revolts of the 1960s, and the motivations and consequences of those impetuous days are still being studied; some groups may have been Maoist-inspired, but most had adequate homegrown bases for their assaults upon what was tirelessly and tiresomely called "the Establishment."

University "A" may or may not emphasize the theory or the philosophy of revolution. So far from being isolated from ongoing social and political affairs, the department of religion at University "A" sees itself as having the same goals as other departments should, and as having no legitimate function in society that does not directly and specifically identify with the current events of given times and places. The prophetic role of the Judeo-Christian tradition is lost in a humorless activism.

University "A" has abandoned an older conception of the university itself. Professors enthusiastically indoctrinate for a "cause." They mount every strategic and tactical weapon of education for change, including revolutionary change, and they do not hesitate to advocate the use of violence when an advantage may be achieved by its use. The classroom becomes the "staff room"—the map room for the barricades. Then one form of politicization tends to beget another. Where there are radicals (revolutionaries) of the right, there will spring up a counter-bloc of professors and "advanced" students who in turn line up their partisans and develop the whole apparatus for counter-propaganda and action on the left. The department and the university no longer serve as centers for understanding, learning, clarification; their resources are given fully and with enthusiasm to sociopolitical effectiveness.

It is admitted that there is no such reality as "pure" teaching, free from all value judgments and biases. Our own biases must be assumed; professors indoctrinate in spite of themselves. Furthermore, it is a legitimate professional peculiarity to have, as Sidney Hook points out, "intellectual concern about the social conditions that bear upon [the student's] activities and that support or frustrate his educational goals." On the other hand, there is a fateful distinction between a relatively objective type of teaching and a dogged propaganda line. Politicizers pass over, even scorn, all the rich purposes and possibilities in education and fall with dull consistency upon devotion to the doctrinaire— doctrinaire even when the goals are all "practical." Hook has taken an uncompromising position against the advocates of politicizing the university. "It is not the teacher's function to indoctrinate his students in behalf of any cause no matter how holy." [7] To be relevant is not necessarily to sell one's soul to a relative, historical end—to absolutize even just and desirable political and economic values. Our prophetic heritage, which calls us to take seriously (that is, to be involved with) the issues that agitate human souls, forbids us to absolutize them or to claim them as the only present obligation.

If University "A" puts its heart, soul and mind into the social, political, and institutional realities, University "B" luxuriates in individualism in religion. There is, among other constants, a sophisticated preoccupation with soul saving—not through preaching that "Jesus saves," but through "the way," the Buddha, Zen, transcendental meditation, and possibly ventures into drugs. Hovering over all is the aura of the mystical, with mostly Oriental props. Devotion to the mysticism of the Orient does not require an analytical, critical approach to the subject matter. Sacred texts, edited for a certain effect, are constantly present, along with movies, slides, and the periodic visit of the holy man. All of these aspects are likely to be presented appreciatively but largely uncritically. Emphasis may be upon "experience"—not always the experience of the classroom student but that of the people whose religion is under examination. "Time" persists as a category mystical in nature, but sidereal time has fallen out of mind like a dream never remembered. The aesthetic is highly prized and exhaustively elaborated. The mood of the department is anti-intellectual but not necessarily obscurantist. There is also, oddly enough, a strong emphasis upon methodology and hermeneutics. There is consistently, however, a wide-ranging distrust of the "relevant" as it may find companionship in society outside the bounds of the institution.

Along with individualistic and mystical concerns, psychologies of various kinds (except behaviorism) flourish in classroom and hallway. There would appear to be indiscriminate obeisance to all religions (except our own), past and present, great and obscure. The occult is not neglected. Witchcraft and sorcery, astrology and numerology receive serious attention. A special occasion featuring almost any kind of religious, psychological, or anthropological novelty will draw a crowd. But try a social or political issue and attendance by both faculty and students will be meager indeed.

There is one exception to the Mars Hill characteristic of the department of religion in this university: the Judeo-Christian tradition is muted and neglected, or "kept in its place," which is subordinate. In fact, as one colleague pointed out in connection with one university, it is clear that at times there is actual hatred of the very tradition (the Judeo-Christian) which fathered and mothered the department and within the context of which the whole departmental venture makes sense in its own culture.

This latter point suggests other consequences. There is hostility to institutional considerations, with the exception of the ritual and the liturgical. This odd hatred of the institutional aspects of religion and education, it will be noted, is never reflected in any prejudice against taking salaries from the institution. Systematic theology, history, and the Judeo-Christian scriptures are placed low on the value scale. The department has grown negative through the years toward an undergraduate major in the Bible, for example. Especially moribund is any possibility of developing a graduate program in the Hebrew-Christian tradition.

Weaving in and out of the fabric of departmental life at University "B" is the titillating notion of doom—the apocalyptic, the eschatological. It is the bass note going boom, boom, doom through the departmental discussions, the dissertations, and much of the "shop talk." Yet there is something ethereal about the fascination with this subject. There is little exposure of students to such realities as are observed in Robert Heilbroner's *An Inquiry into the Human Prospect,* or in Geoffrey Barraclough's writings or even in the less immediately threatening conclusions of the Club of Rome, to say nothing of prospective cataclysms in war and ecological disasters. Eschatology would appear to have nothing to do with any act on the part of God or man; it would appear to have no relationship to linear time or to history.

Students at University "B" suffer the distortion of a preoccupation with individuals or individualism, while the social and cultural dimensions of religion are unknown or unappreciated. Even Alfred North Whitehead did not feel it necessary or desirable to keep his definition of religion to himself. "Religion is what the individual does with his own solitariness," said Whitehead. He had to have an audience to affirm what he declared needed no audience. Dietrich Bonhoeffer expressed the point this way: "God does not intend the history of single persons, but God intends the history of the community of persons." [8] The one-to-one relationship between God and man and between man and man is in contrast to a concern for the welfare of community and society. We need only recall that it was the pervasive preoccupation with "doing one's thing" that helped to ensure that the German universities (including theological faculties) would almost universally embrace Nazism. One notable American theologian has often remarked that a consistent regimen of reading and study can be socially and politically decisive. If he were seeking to foster a fascist regime, he says, he would establish foundations across the land to encourage the study of Kierkegaard, or Bultmann, or Heidegger, or all three. He could then run the country as he pleased, recalling Max Weber's observation that the Prussian reactionaries in Berlin were delighted that so many Germans belonged to singing academies. The na-

tional energies could then be drained off in "warbling." The
Prussian authorities could count on the Germans to be "good
citizens," and this meant passive, nonparticipating citizens.

A corrective approach in the social dimension of religion
was suggested seventy years ago by George Albert Coe. Coe said
that half a seminarian's curriculum should be in the social
sciences. Does such a judgment have any pertinence for majors
in religion and especially for graduate students in university departments of religion? Boston University offers another type of
option, requiring the social science faculty to teach a certain
number of courses in the School of Theology. The theological
faculty, in turn, is required to teach religion courses in the general curriculum.

An unrelieved emphasis upon religious individualism, whatever form or content it has, leads to pessimism and nihilism in
terms of world affirmation, of the meaning of history, and finally
of the significance of the individual for whom religion was so reduced in the first place. Centering on the problem another way,
Abraham Heschel, speaking particularly about the pride and
vanity of contemporary man observes: "It is ironic that the natural sciences have long since abandoned the assumption that
man is the center of nature and ultimate end of the evolutionary
process, but that we still regard it as unnatural, even incon-
ceivable, for man not to act primarily in his own interests in
human relations. Having left scientific anthropocentricity behind,
we cling to egocentricity in religion and morality." [9]

Perhaps it is fair to say that departments of religion might well
become agents in what Thomas R. Wolanin calls the "policy
arena." Government policymaking in higher education has direct bearing on students, particularly graduate students in religion. Critical examination of government policy, in its effect
upon education and society as a whole, ought to be a consistent
part of the vocation of departments of religion. It should be
emphasized again, however, that fruitful concern with social
policy is a group affair and does not always mean that each
person expresses discrete judgments or takes responsible actions.
Education should engender both an awareness of the significance
of groups and a sense of responsibility for participation in groups

concerned with social policy. Correcting the politicizing of University "A" cannot justify the companion error of unrelieved individualism. "It is through group participation that sensitivity and commitment to values are given institutional expression; it is through groups that social power is organized. . . . It is through groups that the cultural atmosphere of a community and a nation is created." [10]

Departments of religion are responsible not only to their own inner being and structure. They are a part of the college or university and of the community in which they exist; they exist not for themselves alone but for society. This would appear to be too obvious a truth to need repeating, but one which residents in the dominion of University "B" have long forgotten.

Both University "A" and University "B" may be reminded that the prophetic element in the heritage of departments of religion calls persistently for engagement of the question of legitimacy. "Legitimacy" is a category native to sociology, and sociologists have followed Max Weber's lead in examining the basis of authority for institutions under this rubric. There are many, and often conflicting, definitions of legitimacy.[11] In terms of the special responsibility of departments of religion to stress the problem of legitimacy, the following definition is useful: legitimacy is "a condition of . . . validity, and acceptance enjoyed by . . . systems of authority with some law, principle, or source of authorization." [12] Prophetic religion consistently raises the question of legitimacy. Institutions, whether political, economic, ecclesiastical, or educational, must always be challenged with regard to their reasons for being and their claim to authority. Religion faculties as academicians and as bearers of the "final claim" owe it to their students and to their communities to foster examination of any and all claims to legitimacy, including those of departments of religion. Two illustrations are suggestive. It is said that a crucifix on the altar in a church in Toronto gives the impression at first blush of being a large question mark. This impression could suggest the question of legitimacy in the church or religion. A. Lawrence Lowell, a famous president of Harvard, used to preach a sermon in which he set forth the thesis that the location of Appleton Chapel (now the Harvard Memorial Church) opposite Widener Library in the Yard says something about the role of religion in raising the question as to what all the learning is about.[13]

Moral Test for Departments of Religion

Affirmative action and hiring policies pose a special question for departments of religion. What the government established as legal policy in Title VII of the 1964 Civil Rights Act should have been, and sometimes was, moral policy for years before. And why should it not have been? What the national government made the law of the nation was in principle a concerted effort to root out racial and sexual injustice. It was by way of "affirmative action" policies on most campuses that justice was projected into operational policy. It would be eminently desirable if it could be said that what the law finally institutionalized had been the policy in principle and practice of departments of religion decades ago, but this cannot be said. Yet "affirmative action" was implicit in departmental convictions about equality and justice. The forces for justice and equality find their bedrock support through the ages: in the Stoics, in Medieval thought, in the witness of the Radical Reformers, and, of course, in the fundamental assumptions of ancient biblical and prophetic religion.

In practice "affirmative action" means, among other things, more investment in time and money in examining a greater number and variety of candidates. The social and educational values to come from such a policy outweigh every major and minor drawback, though this proposition would not be agreed to universally by any means.

Departments of religion, especially, have to stand for a variety of values. In questions of affirmative action "equality" is, for example, a social and legal category, as well as a religious and moral one. The prophetic-critical obligation still binding departments of religion requires that the limitations of "equality," as an absolute, be clearly recognized and yet not be allowed to become excuses to subvert affirmative action policies.

It cannot be "affirmed" and acted upon too often that all avenues must be opened to all qualified persons. But a decent application of critical faculties and principles must lead to a conclusion at some points that "affirmative action" as literally interpreted does not make sense in all situations. For example, suppose a department had an opportunity to hire such a candidate as Paul Tillich, Martin Buber, Reinhold Niebuhr, Karl Barth, James L. Adams, Herbert Marcuse, Hannah Arendt, or other equally eminent persons of the past or present. Should such a candidate be rejected in favor of a lesser scholar and personage? There is no way the principle of "equality" can be absolutely operative. The procedure may be gone through to satisfy the technicalities of the law, but the exercise would be an empty and hypocritical one. Sidney Hook and others have emphasized the necessity of providing the kind of social and educational environment that would permit all an equal opportunity to qualify for positions. However, what we are dealing with here is really not a matter of "equal qualifications." We are dealing with incommensurability, not calculable degrees of qualification. Did anyone ever try to apply "affirmative action" criteria to Paul Tillich or Reinhold Niebuhr in relationship to other candidates for a position?

Perhaps the ultimate reduction derivable from affirmative action was advocated recently by Caroline Bird. Speaking of colleges and universities she said: "Still another way to inject sanity into job-filling is to extend existing laws prohibiting discrimination on the basis of race, religion, sex and age to *prohibit discrimination on the basis of educational attainment, too*" (italics added). If she means simply an empty matching of academic degree with degree, she may have a point. But the article does not suggest that this is her meaning.[14]

In the end, however, a department of religion cannot forget the part of its tradition that calls for love (agape) as well as justice and due consideration for incommensurability. Special needs, in principle, require special considerations—not the same treatment. Under this moral imperative special needs may require a woman or a black person. But special considerations, requirements, or needs may also at times come in white skin. The burden of proof, though, is upon the white-male-dominated departments of religion.

At some point the problem of fairness and tenure has to be

noted. Opposition to affirmative action policies in this area sometimes reflects serious concern for academic freedom, as well as for human rights, equal rights, due process, and the possibility of "reverse discrimination." It is no doubt true also that tenure can be a bulwark for the entrenched white male. It becomes here a question of the willingness to venture—to venture into an open examination of our privilege and power of tenure. Malcolm Sherman suggests the vulnerability of many faculty members in the way their tenure is defended. In the past, he points out, older men have sought to show their vigor and patriotism by sending young men off to the wars; "So some tenured white male faculty [have] sought to prove something by their willingness to assign jobs held by younger men to women and minorities." [15] Bearers of the "final claim" could find the resources for a self-critical approach to the issues surrounding tenure.

If this paper appears quite critical of departments of religion, this is no accident. The subject matter of this volume lends itself to the raising of critical questions. Departments of religion stand in a unique relationship to the subject matter of this volume. In terms of scholarship and quality of teaching, departments of religion generally compare favorably with other departments in our colleges and universities. But in terms of power elements in the schools and society at large, departments of religion hold not only special opportunities but also special responsibilities. These departments may be said to operate under a particular application of the biblical word: "To whom much is given, of him shall much be required."

NOTES

1. Ronald H. Bohr, "Social Power: A Missing Dimension in the Scientific Study of Religion" (Paper presented at the meeting of the Society for the Scientific Study of Religion, Montreal, October 1968), p. 1; some of these analyses are: James Luther Adams, "What Kind of Religion Has a Place in Higher Education?" *Journal of Bible and Religion* 13, no. 4 (November 1945): 184–92; Martha Biehle, ed., *Fifty Years, 1923–1973: A Brief History of the National Council on Religion in Higher Education and the Society for Religion in*

Higher Education (New Haven, Conn.: Society for Values in Higher Education, 1974); Merrimon Cuninggim, *The College Seeks Religion* (New Haven, Conn.: Yale University Press, 1945), chapter 10; Ray Hart, *Religious Studies in State University of New York* (Stony Brook: State University of New York, 1975); Karl Hartzell and Harrison Sasscer, *The Study of Religion on the Campus of Today* (Washington, D. C.: Association of American Colleges, 1967); Samuel Hill, "The Teaching of Religion in the State University," *Review and Expositor* 69, no. 3 (1972): 335–46; Milton D. McLean, *Religion Studies in Public Universities* (Carbondale: Southern Illinois University Press, 1967); Robert Michaelsen, *The Study of Religion in American Universities* (New Haven, Conn.: Society for Religion in Higher Education, 1965); Ramsey and Wilson, *The Study of Religion in Colleges and Universities* (Princeton, N.J.: Princeton University Press, 1970); Claude Welch, *Graduate Education in Religion* (Missoula: University of Montana Press, 1971); Claude Welch, *Religion in the Undergraduate Curriculum* (Washington, D.C.: Association of American Colleges, 1972).

2. Adams, "What Kind of Religion," p. 185 (used with permission of the author).

3. See Preface for this conception of power.

4. Adams, "What Kind of Religion," p. 185.

5. "Contribution to the Critique of Hegel's Philosophy of Right," in Karl Marx and Friederich Engels, *On Religion* (New York: Schocken Books, 1964), p. 41; Niebuhr, ibid., p. vii.

6. Ramsbey, "Ordained Protestant Professor," p. 290.

7. Sidney Hook, "Don't Politicize the University," *Review World* 1, no. 9 (January 12, 1974): 64.

8. Alfred North Whitehead, *Religion in the Making* (New York: Macmillan Co., 1927), p. 16; Dietrich Bonhoeffer, *Sanctorum Communio* (Munich: Chr. Kaiser Verlag, 1954), p. 52.

9. Abraham J. Heschel, *A Passion for Truth* (New York: Farrar, Straus & Giroux, 1973), p. 316.

10. Thomas R. Wolanin, "Federal Policy Making in Higher Education," *AAUP Bulletin* 61, no. 4 (December 1975): 309–14; James Luther Adams, "Centerstance: An Essay on the Purposes of a Liberal Arts Education," *The Liberal Context* 2, no. 1 (Winter 1962): 11.

11. See John H. Schaar, "Legitimacy in the Modern State," in Philip Green and Sanford Levinson, eds., *Power and Community: Dissenting Essays in Political Science* (New York: Random House, 1969), pp. 282–86.

12. Robert Bierstedy, "Legitimacy," in Julius Gould and William L. Kolb, eds., *A Dictionary of the Social Sciences* (New York: Free Press of Glencoe, 1964), p. 386.

13. As told by James Luther Adams.

14. Caroline Bird, "Out of Academic Ghettoes, into the Mainstream," *The New York Times,* March 15, 1975, p. 27. A similar suggestion was made in the discussions at the State University of New York at Albany. Sherman, "Affirmative Action and the AAUP," *AAUP Bulletin* 61, no. 4 (December 1975): 294.

15. Sherman, "Affirmative Action," p. 295.

Images of Power in Academia:
A Critical View

GARY W. SYKES

As the political trauma known as Watergate recedes from every-day consciousness, there appears a tendency to dismiss it as an anomaly or a curious flaw in the administration of former President Richard Nixon. From the earliest beginnings of the crisis, most Americans refused to accept the possibility that the highest circles of American government would conspire to tamper with the electoral process, burglarize the headquarters of the opposition party, use the FBI, CIA, and the IRS for political gain, and so on. Most citizens had to be forced to this realization by a deluge of overwhelming evidence, and there is still the nagging suspicion that if the famous tape transcripts had not been part of the evidence the president would not have been forced to resign. In short, the events called Watergate ran counter to most people's expectations about the nature of leadership in America.

A few, however, expressed different ideas about the abuse of power and were not surprised by the events, though they were surprised by the magnitude of what happened as well as by the difficulty in proving culpability. One noted political scientist said that "to believe Watergate was unique in American politics, one must be either naïve or partisan." Those expressing this point of view are part of a long tradition in America—some might call it the Jeffersonian tradition—which understands that power inherently involves a risk of abuse. This traditional view of democracy has always maintained that citizens must be suspicious, even cynical, in their estimates of those in power.

How can the apparent naïveté of those who see Watergate as unique be understood? What images of leadership have come to dominate our national consciousness in the past few decades? These questions raise complex issues beyond the scope of this article. To talk about formation of political perceptions can involve psychological, sociological, and political theories that play a role in the construction of political reality. This paper is more modest; it looks at the images of political leaders fostered in textbooks, scholarly writings, and everyday journalism. It cannot provide evidence about why leadership images change, but it can discuss different images that dominate in the interpretation of political events. This article argues that many scholars in American colleges and universities apparently have lost the Jeffersonian fear once part of the liberal heritage, and that this fear has been replaced by a more benign image of political power in American politics. For whatever reason, contemporary writers tend to idealize American politics and elevate its leaders to positions of authority that might have frightened earlier democratic political thinkers.

Briefly, this article outlines what appears to be a prevailing view of the nature of political leadership fostered by university scholars. It argues that in recent years important political thinkers have defined American political leadership in such a way as to create expectations which do not reflect some traditional concerns about the malevolent uses of power. Although it might be unfair to say that conventional theories have rationalized the professional leader or that they have constructed an apologia for established interests, this article does document a gradual erosion of traditional democratic concerns in favor of an idea of democracy based on procedure and efficiency. The cost of this erosion, from traditional democracy to proceduralism, may be the loss of the critical role scholarship often plays in analyzing the nature of political experience. Political theories in recent years assume that threats to democratic order come essentially from lower and marginal social and economic groups, not from the leadership strata. Watergate, and all its ramifications, was largely unexpected in the deluge of research which celebrated the virtues of American political leaders.

Three decades ago, Harold Lasswell in his classic book about political power described men who sought power in a way pregnant with the possibility for renewing the study of politics. Power, he argued, was a relationship of "giving and taking," and its participants were subject to sanctions to ensure their performance. He used the term *political power* to designate a situation in which "severe deprivations are expected to follow the breach of a pattern of conduct." [1]

Lasswell was concerned with the abnormal propensity of leaders to seek power as an instrumental goal in serving ego needs. The pursuit of power was understood "as a compensatory reaction against [a] low estimate of self; and the reaction occurs when opportunities exist both for the displacement of ungratified craving from the primary circle to public targets and for the rationalization of these displacements in the public interest." [2]

The goal of democratic societies, for Lasswell, included a commitment to freedom that ultimately meant the elimination of power, though he admitted this to be utopian. The radical democrat (i.e., the anarchist), he concluded, desires to eliminate leaders, but the probability of reducing power to the vanishing point seems very remote. In the advancement of this goal, however, Lasswell suggested that through education (i.e., appropriate socialization) democratic personalities may flourish. It was the active and responsible citizen, open and tolerant, believing in human dignity, and subordinating power drives to the interest of the commonwealth, who deserved to achieve a position of leadership. Leaders of this type, Lasswell contended, help us advance toward a democratic society, or at least help us toward the removal of power from politics. "Progressive democratization, therefore, calls for the formation of a democratic personality, which is a process of developing character, technique, and perspective. As a guide to science and politics, society needs self-observatories capable of exposing the truth about the hidden destructiveness of our cultural institutions, and of reporting on the effect of experimental efforts at reformation." [3]

In sum, Lasswell suggested that many who, because of their own psychological needs, seek power and the ability to impose sanctions, will use that power for destructive purposes. Notice that Lasswell did not presume that democracy had become a reality, or that civic virtue in a democratic culture prevailed. His definition of political leadership did not deny the possibility of "exposing the truth about the hidden destructiveness of our cultural institutions." His perspective led him to talk about the "garrison state," militarism, and political power as repressive forces against democratic values associated with openness, tolerance, and human dignity.

Many of Lasswell's colleagues have ignored much of his theory. Consequently, contemporary writers often conclude that political officeholders act as representatives of the public interest, play a professional role, and protect democratic values. Thus they often characterize American politics not as an institution advancing toward utopian democratic goals but as a democratic "reality." In doing so, these writers de-emphasize the power aspect of politics in favor of a democratic theory celebrating stability and a system of accountability (procedural or process democracy).[4]

The achievement of democracy, for Lasswell, was problematic, given the propensity of some officeholders to impose their ego needs on the public situation. Therefore constant vigilance, questioning, and criticism were essential to prevent leadership elements from destroying democratic values. Political scholars in recent years have largely ignored much of Lasswell's work and proceeded to rationalize power and its distribution in American politics. The emergence of this view is connected with many interrelated and complex issues, including changes in epistemology related to the scientific or technological revolution. This article, however, limits itself to discussing changes in democratic theory resulting from prevalent academic views of American political leaders, especially the functional role in which they are seen as representatives of the public interest.

The power personality Lasswell describes resembles the "authoritarian personality" in social science literature. He contrasts the democratic personality, described as one committed to values other than rulership itself, with the power personality, which is pathological. Presumably, the difference, or at least one difference, between democratic and authoritarian politics rests on the purposes for which power is used. Power in the former is exercised as an instrument by which to achieve values consistent with democratic culture, while the exercise of power in the latter represents ego gratification, protection of elite interests, or a desire to compensate for pathology. Procedural democracy, the theory of democracy which emerged shortly after Lasswell's study, excludes widespread participation and citizen competence in favor of a system of organizational equilibrium among dominant professional leaders within the social order. The role of political leaders most often described is not one of the exercise of power on behalf of a social or economic class, nor does it concern the potential for power exercised for self-interest; rather the prevailing view describes leaders as professional brokers among competing interests.[5]

Many studies conclude that persons seeking power in American politics ultimately express characteristics of the democratic personality—that is, they are open and tolerant to the extent they can be instrumental in resolving conflicts among competing groups and interests. They are believed to share a commitment to a "democratic creed" or the "rules of the game" as part of an abstract democratic consensus. Thus the social fabric of American politics is said to be undergirded by a societal consensus about democratic norms, at least among the leadership strata.

The process or procedural theory of democracy has achieved salience among scholars and in most textbooks; it has also filtered into the conventional wisdom of society at large. A debate has continued, however, between those who define democracy as procedural (emphasis on the process of policymaking rather than on its ends) and those who take the more traditional view, here called reformist, in the Lasswellian sense that sees democratic development as incomplete. This debate is yet to be resolved.[6]

In defining democracy as procedural, well-known scholars such as Gabriel Almond, Sidney Verba, Robert Dahl, Seymour Lipset, and Anthony Downs distinguish democratic and nondemocratic institutions, using such criteria as electoral openness, cultural requisites, and social and economic development, rather than more traditional criteria such as equality, freedom, and effective participation.[7] For example: "To avoid ethical premises, we define democratic government descriptively, i.e., by enumerating certain characteristics which *in practice* distinguish this form of government from others."[8]

The characteristics Downs refers to are the following: popular elections held periodically, set terms of office not to be altered during an incumbent's term (constitutionalism), and universal adult suffrage. Downs avoids discussing the presumptions upon which selection of these democratic indicators is based. His definition of democracy is apparently drawn from the prevailing reality. It appears that a major presumption of the process model of democracy, which stresses accountability over "normative" criteria, is that American institutions have achieved democratic goals. Without discussing democratic values, examining only manifest processes, many of these writers conduct studies of voting behavior, elections, socioeconomic requisites, competition, and so on, all drawn from the United States as an indication of the workings of American democracy.

The process definition of democracy does not include characteristics such as widespread citizen participation, policy effectiveness, or equality (except procedural equality) often associated with traditional democracy.[9] Whether or not these characteristics are relevant is another question that cannot be dealt with here, but the presumption seems implicit that describing democratic society is tantamount to describing the practices of American politics.

The role defined for political leaders in process democracy differs significantly from their role under traditional theories of democracy. Lasswell in talking about power is concerned with its abuse and the tendency some leaders might have to use it for their own ends. He argues for the creation of an active, informed citizenry and greater participation for all groups. However, the following passage about reconciling power and responsiveness by Almond and Verba stands in contrast:

> The tension between governmental power and responsiveness has a parallel in the conflicting demands made upon the citizens of a democratic system. Certain

things are demanded of the ordinary citizen if elites are
to be responsive to him: the ordinary citizen must express
his point of view so that elites can know what he wants;
he must be involved in politics so that he will know and
care whether or not elites are being responsive, and he
must be influential so as to enforce responsive behavior
by the elites. In other words, elite responsiveness requires that the ordinary citizens act according to the
rationality-activist model of citizenship [traditional democratic theory]. But if the alternate role of elite power is
to be achieved, quite contradictory attitudes and behavior are to be expected of the ordinary man. If elites
are to be powerful and make authoritative decisions, then
the involvement, activity, and *influence of the ordinary
man must be limited*. The ordinary citizen must turn
power over to elites and let them rule. The need for elite
power requires that the ordinary citizen be relatively
passive, uninvolved, and deferential to elites.[10]

Lasswell saw freedom as a goal to be achieved even though
he was cautious about the likelihood of its achievement. Leaders,
from the point of view of Almond and Verba, are necessary,
functional *decision-makers* who respond to citizen inputs, but
who must be free to implement these inputs.[11] There is little
concern about the possibility of pathology in politics. Power-
holders do not rule; they make decisions in response to citizen
needs and system requisites, and they must have freedom to
achieve their goals, goals presumably consistent with the functional role they perform. In other words, there is an inversion in
thinking about leadership. In traditional democratic theory
political power was viewed with suspicion and elites were to be
watched for the corrupting influences of power, if not pathological tendencies. What Almond and Verba suggest is that elites
must be free. We find we are discussing freedom for elites and
the necessity for citizen deference, noninvolvement, and passivity.

In response to expected criticisms of their redefinition of
democracy, Almond and Verba reply that finding discrepancies
between the ideals of traditional democracy and research find-
ings should not be taken as "evidence for the malfunctioning of

democracy." Rather, they argue, the difference is there because standards have been set "unreasonably high." A more useful task "would be to hold the view that theories of politics should be drawn from the realities of political life." [12] In other words, since political leaders and passive citizens in American politics are found to lack characteristics associated with traditional ideals, researchers should attempt to understand the extant processes in order to understand democracy. It is not surprising to find that democracy comes to mean for the authors something less than the achievement of politics without self-serving power-wielders; it is seen primarily as a system of accountability which justifies elite maneuverability rather than a participatory polity in which collective decisions are made.

To build a stronger argument about the pervasiveness of this view of democratic leaders, the remainder of this essay deals with three distinct aspects of the prevailing role defined for leaders. First is the brokerage role, defining elites as functional components in a bargaining arrangement based on agreement about "game rules." The image of leadership is one in which professional decision-makers, socialized into the prevailing democratic consensus, maintain a commitment to values such as openness, tolerance, and fair play as they perform essential functions consistent with these values.

Second, this essay will follow implications of the functional view of leaders and find that successful role performance is associated with certain skills and educational experiences of a process of professionalization through which the leader is seen as "expert." The role of the expert is said to demand certain skills and knowledge nourished in specific strata within society. Since ordinary citizens are said to lack basic competence, they are found to lack "substantial rationality." This supposed inadequacy is often interpreted to provide a justification for the bias in leadership selection; it also generates a fear that the ordinary citizen, if aroused, may threaten democratic institutions.

Finally this discussion will evaluate critically the literature dealing with many democratic-attitude studies and opinion studies in which it is found that leaders are more committed than are ordinary citizens to procedural democracy and serve as protectors of "rational politics." The ultimate goal of this literature, it appears, is to convince the reader that leaders are not power-oriented in the traditional sense. It will be argued that this view describes a political order in which power is almost nonexistent—where politics is described as a game being played. But the question remains: What about Watergate?

Gabriel Almond describes in broad terms the institutional role structure defined by Anglo-American political culture.[13] This culture he describes as secular, meaning multivalued, and emancipated from traditionalism; however, it is also homogenous in that values involving ends and means are shared within society. This value-consensus defines role expectations for political leaders and provides for a functional understanding of their activity. "Holders of office in the formal-legal role structure tend to be viewed," he says, "as agents and instrumentalities, or as brokers occupying points in the bargaining process." Because there are low levels of anxiety about political outcomes due to the shared agreement over ends and means, politics takes on the "atmosphere of a game." Indeed, he argues that "fun" is frequently an aspect of the bargaining and coalition building among leaders and their constituencies.

Other political scientists expressing a similar view of the functional role of leadership have produced an impressive array of studies substantiating this view of political leadership. It is impossible to mention all subsequent studies appearing to reflect this view, but a few of the most visible should demonstrate that Almond may have been correct in asserting that this analytical framework could have the standing of a "paradigm" in the social sciences.

In his now classic book on the presidency, Richard Neustadt argues that to understand the role of this highest political leader requires study not of the formal power structure, but of the officeholder's personal ability to influence.[14] Presidential leadership does not rest primarily on power, in this view, but on the ability to use resources of the office in the pluralist bargaining situation that, Almond suggests, characterizes diffused, homogenous-secular political culture. In fact, Neustadt considers the concept of "clerk" as an important description of the role of the chief executive. He describes the presidency as an instrumentality which can be used extensively to enhance the incumbent's bargaining capacity with power blocs in the national political structure. He concludes his study by arguing that we need a president who is an "expert" in understanding this subtle and complex structure of influence to achieve success for his policy goals.

Neustadt's description may be very helpful in understanding conflicts that emerge among leaders at the national level, but other aspects of the executive role are not expressed very clearly by this theory of leadership behavior. Neustadt does not deal explicitly with origins and consequences of policy goals selected by presidential leaders. The president may bargain, persuade, or cajole congressional leaders in support of policy goals, but implementation of their agreement may mean disaster for either underrepresented or excluded groups. In other words, latent consequences of compromise made among dominant interests in performing their functional role by solving conflict may have secondary or tertiary impact on others not directly involved in the "game" itself.[15] Thus the ultimate effect of successful persuasion as an aspect of presidential power can, and often does, have coercive effects on other groups within the social order. To describe the president's power as the power to persuade examines only the process, not the impact, of how that office alters activity within the society.

Game is a word often used to describe "secular-homogenous" politics and may be misleading, because noncontestants may not be immune from the outcome. The metaphor of a game usually implies that contestants agree about the rules. In politics, however, some groups are able to change the rules, while other groups are not. This metaphor creates a more benign image of political leadership than might be held by groups at the lower end of the power spectrum.

One other example should suffice to indicate the extent to which the view of functional elites with primarily persuasive power is widespread among contemporary students of American politics. In his book on the United States Senate, Donald Mathews presents the clearest expression of how common this perspective is among those describing the workings of established institutions.[16] Mathews tries to identify various factors in the recruitment processes that promote or diminish the likelihood of the Senate's achieving statistical representation of various social, economic, and cultural groups. Not surprisingly he finds the Senate an unrepresentative body in terms of its members' social and economic backgrounds. He identifies various characteristics of the different states as either barriers or advantages depending on factors such as the candidate's age, sex, religion, race, and social class. Legislative roles and underlying norms also contribute to the likelihood of success for a candidate. His data suggest the existence of a recruitment bias ensuring that senators are elected from specific demographic backgrounds; the data also suggest that this may be conducive to successful adaptation to senatorial norms.

Mathews concludes that the Senate generally recruits politically experienced upper-middle-class professionals who are male, Protestant, and white. Insofar as this selection apparatus is operative, it suggests that the Senate is an unrepresentative body, since many cultural and economic groups in the society are unlikely to achieve direct representation.

Mathews has outlined paths of selection for a political "elite" in the Lasswellian sense (not everyone in the society has a relatively equal chance for election to leadership positions). But Mathews makes it clear that even though there is a decidedly unrepresentative flavor to the Senate, many incumbents belie their "patrician" background by playing the role of "intercessor" or advocate for interests not represented. The brokerage role of political leaders is not severely questioned in Mathews's work, even though he presents little evidence that this role is actually played by many in Congress. Certain political types he calls "professionals" actually do most of the work within the legislative institution. He estimates that less than 5 percent of the adult population has a chance to be elected to the Senate, but he does not despair, because those elected are the best of American civilization.

> The senators were selected, with only rare exceptions, from near the top of the society's class system. . . . While this conclusion rings harsh in many an American democrat's ear, it should not be a particularly surprising con-

clusion. A stratified society places different evaluation on various social positions, and the prestige of the office or position tends to be transferred to the person who fills it. Thus the bank president or lawyer is a "better" man than the janitor or policeman. As long as the system or stratification in a society is generally accepted [by consensus], one must expect people to look for political leadership toward those who have met the current definition of success and hence are considered worthy individuals. Voters seem to prefer candidates who are not like themselves but are what they would like to be.[17]

In overall terms, while the data might convince the observer that the Senate is a conglomeration of middle- and upper-class representatives, Mathews concludes that the role of the senator, because of the enlightenment and expertise of those who occupy this position of power and leadership, is given to men socially accepted as the most talented in playing the role of leader. They are representative because they are symbols of what the average person would like to be. They are legitimate because the class system from which they are drawn is legitimate. Political leaders are not self-seeking powermongers in the Lasswellian sense, nor are they representatives of a ruling class; they are professionals committed to adjudicating, compromising, and bargaining among constituent elements, and they play a functional "democratic" role. They deserve our deference because they possess knowledge and expertise essential in a complex social order.

Accordingly, Mathews is not the first to suggest that political leaders perform a functional role. Political leaders lead via their expertise in acting as brokers. Rather than being articulators of dominant class values, they are seen as agents or instrumentalities divorced from ideology. The suggestion that political leaders are experts without ideology (or professionals) will be discussed in detail below.

The image, at least, of leadership that emerges from this brief and selective overview is substantially different from the one projected by traditional democratic ideals. That view, emphasizing the necessity for constant vigilance to protect from the abuse of political power, is replaced by the image of the political leader as technician, as skillful game-player, and as the carrier of democratic civilization. The Lasswellian concern over psycho-pathology in politics is barely visible. Accordingly, the assumption that power relationships have sanctions as an inherent ingredient and the belief that a political class is an ever-present threat are drowned out by the approving roar from the spectators.

Functional rationality, says Karl Mannheim, involves coordination of activities and behavior to achieve specific ends or goals. Substantial rationality, on the other hand, involves "intelligent insight" into the complexity of a situation, independent understanding that allows for intelligent thought, and by implication the ability to rise above immediate constraints in order to make an independent judgment of the whole. The problem for modern societies, as he sees it, is that "the more industrialized a society is and the more advanced its division of labour and organization, the greater will be the number of spheres of human activity which will be [merely] functionally rational." In this situation, according to Mannheim, "a few people can see things more and more clearly over an ever-widening field, while the average man's capacity for rational judgment steadily declines once he has turned over to the organizer the responsibility for making decisions." [18] The results are an increasing distance between leader and follower, surrender of individuality because of increasing interdependence and rationalized complexity, and elevation of organizers to key positions in society as leaders whose interpretations of events take precedence over other interpretations.

Much of Mannheim's thesis has been accepted as a forthright description of politics in industrial society and may actually represent a set of conventional assumptions for many. Though the language varies and the political perspectives shift, this view of modern rationality is present in the literature which emphasizes the "end of ideology" and the professional-expert leadership role.

William Kornhauser in his discussion of mass society and democratic politics suggests that the impact of modernization on large-scale societies can be summed up in the word *atomization*, or in Mannheim's terminology, increasing functional rationality. One effect of modernization is creation of a climate for mass movements led by men themselves victims of atomization.[19] However, industrialization is also said to create certain contexts that socialize leaders so that social and political experiences insulate them from effects of industrialization itself and give them values of liberal democracy to temper their quest for power. Liberal democratic pluralism, he maintains, creates the possibility that leaders will be vulnerable to the masses, but it also tempers this vulnerability through stratification creating a "necessary tension between elites and non-elites." The "nihilism" of the masses, he continues, threatens liberal democracy more than tensions created by mass differences such as class antagonisms. To avoid mass-society politics, Kornhauser suggests the need for a multiplicity of nonalienating, nonatomizing leadership subcultures. He stresses the need to encourage social pluralism among leaders to overcome the disintegrating effects of modernization. Competing leaders, located within the group structure of liberal societies, will provide the missing element democratic theory overlooks in its attempt to make leaders accountable and therefore vulnerable. Kornhauser's democratic theory consequently discusses the need to protect leaders from the masses, rather than the need to make leaders more responsive to citizens or to protect citizens from the abuse of power.

An incomplete outline of the theory of functional expertise emerges in Kornhauser's work. The leadership subculture provides for competition and accountability as hallmarks of liberal democracy. But leaders must be insulated from atomizing trends of modern society by the presence of "a plurality of independent groups" from which they are chosen as leaders. As Kornhauser succinctly puts it, "A plurality of independent and limited-function groups [social and economic pluralism in the private sphere] supports liberal democracy by providing social bases of free and open competition for leadership, widespread participation in the selection of leaders, restraint in the application of pressures on leaders, and self-government in wide areas of social life. Therefore, where social pluralism is strong, liberty and democracy tend to be strong." Kornhauser appears implicitly to ask: How can democracy in the modern world be protected

from the people? His answer: By allowing substantial independence for groups from which leaders are drawn so they do not
experience the atomization of industrial society. "There must be
extensive opportunities for elites to formulate policies and take
action without *ad hoc* interference from the outside." [20]

Kornhauser (as well as other writers, such as David Truman)
attempts to construct a political theory stressing the integrating
role of secondary groups against the "disintegrating" effects of
mass movements and mass politics.

Kornhauser's view is echoed by Giuseppe Di Palma. In the
United States, Di Palma says, participation is a function of the
individual's position in the society and his consequent attitudes
toward prevailing political values. "Certain kinds of people, by
virtue of their training and position in society, are in relatively
better positions to hear and be heard as individuals. This is
especially true for professional leaders in government, in business, and, to a lesser extent, in labor—men who are believed to
be and consider themselves qualified to head up major institutions by virtue of their education and training. It is also true for
the rapidly increasing proportion of the population that is
receiving a higher education and going into professional occu-
pations." [21] In other words, those "substantially rational" by virtue of their education and professionalism are to be nurtured
through a social pluralism that trains them as democratic leaders. Other theorists must develop more completely the characteristic of elite independence as a necessary prerequisite for
roles as professional leaders who act as functional agents.

Kornhauser's representative work expresses a significant
ambivalence toward democratic values that emerges elsewhere
in the literature: "We see participation as the expression and
product of a person's integration into the system of social and
political relations. Participation does not flourish unless the
citizen, by reason of his privileged position in society or of his
trusting and effective relation to the polity, finds it easy or
advantageous to work within the existing political framework.
. . . one can say that those who participate in politics are more
able and *willing* to work within its present frame, to *accept* its
basic rules, and to be *interested* in its current outputs than those
who do not participate." [22] What Kornhauser points out and

others suggest is that those who preserve these values in the civic culture are primarily the educated groups. They have the skills, motivations, and opportunities and are exposed to group pressures inducing them to participate.

The ambivalence many writers express is that democratic theory embraces a belief in citizen competence, while modern industrial development, as they see it, denies most citizens the capacity to rule. Consequently, professional leaders are singled out as best equipped to rule. The problem is to make them accountable, and process democracy accomplishes this by defining for these individuals a responsive brokerage role that appears free from ideology, while at the same time they are said to be committed to values of liberal democratic culture as "rules of the game."

Robert Dahl's book on New Haven politics summarizes this view of political leaders by elevating them to the role of professionals. The professional, identified by opportunities, motivations, and especially by skills in using available influence-resources in the "art" of politics, is said to be "more familiar with the democratic norms, more consistent, . . . more detailed, and explicit in [his] political attitudes, and more completely in agreement on the norms." [23] The politico has skill in what Dahl calls the art of pyramiding, that is, transforming petty sovereignties (polyarchic arrays of groups) into executive-centered coalitions to achieve results, providing nonpoliticos (the slack in the arrangement) do not interfere. Leaders are mobilizers, influencers, skillful role players, as well as the most democratic members of society. They increase the chances of stable politics because elites are accountable to the "creed" as well as to their particular constituencies.

"Most citizens," says Dahl, "assume that the American political system is consistent with the democratic creed. Indeed, the common view seems to be that our system is not only democratic but is perhaps the most perfect expression of democracy that exists anywhere." This belief is sustained and reinforced through education and very powerful processes of socialization. A major problem, however, is that the average person is unlikely to permit democratic values to be consistently interpreted in concrete situations. The political stratum, on the other hand, protects and defends the "creed" as applied in specific instances because they "have on the average considerably more formal education than the population as a whole, [and] they have been more thoroughly exposed to the creed and its implications." [24] Because they have a greater commitment to democratic norms, Dahl calls the professionals democratic legitimists. They do not challenge basic beliefs, and in fact they lead the average citizen in the application of these beliefs—that is, leaders appear to have the Mannheimian characteristic of "substantial rationality"; they see more clearly the consequences of their actions and protect the edifice within which rational or democratic behavior can occur.

This view clearly presents a situation in which political professionals guide, shape, and protect the democratic process. Fortunately, "the fact that a large number of citizens do not believe in the political norms actually applied, particularly extending political liberties to unpopular individuals and groups, has slight effect on the outcome." [25] The professionals in accomplishing their task perform with skill and education born of years in the gristmill of politics; they are said to understand what has to be done and they can do it (i.e., they possess substantial rationality). The professional in this view is the pivot of American democracy: he believes in political norms that are democratic; he responds in ways that do not violate those norms; and in the end his skillful role-playing as coalition-builder within the political stratum protects democracy from the people. The form of democratic politics Dahl describes may not satisfy traditional democrats, but it does recognize the reality of politics. It is "unfortunate" that citizens are not competent to govern intelligently, says Dahl, but it is fortunate that leaders are.

The slack in this system, that reservoir filled with average people, remains relatively passive and acquiescent. As Dahl points out: "The existence of a great deal of political slack seems to be a characteristic of pluralistic political systems and the liberal societies in which these systems operate. In liberal societies, politics is a sideshow in the great circus of life." [26]

It is a game in which most are spectators. However, Dahl does not emphasize the aspects of politics that involve the threat of force, actual coercion, or the use of institutional violence. Negotiating and bargaining may be part of the political world he describes, but this world may also include the self-serving holding of power. What Dahl seems to describe is what Heinz Eulau labeled as the "politics of happiness." Politics may be a game or a circus from certain vantage points, but the impact of political decisions and their implementation may not always be benign. Even though the decision-making process may be pluralistic and procedurally democratic, it does not follow that decisions are either interpreted democratically or carried out without abuse of power.

If the argument to this point accurately describes the contemporary academic image of American political leadership, it would be incomplete unless the conclusion hinted at—that leaders are seen to embody the "democratic personality"—could be found in many studies of political attitudes. What emerges from a brief examination of the literature on leader- and nonleader-attitudes and opinions is the idea that leaders are more "democratic" than followers, and that they are intellectually better equipped to make decisions than the average person.

A well-known earlier work by Samuel Stouffer is one of the first major studies that have contributed significantly to the attitudinal literature on the democratic personality.[27] Stouffer finds that community leaders who reply to questions about the extension of civil rights to nonconformists, such as communists and atheists, are more tolerant and more likely to support democratic ideals than average individuals within the community studied. Even leaders in the more "conservative" groups are found to give greater support to civil liberties than the average nonleader.

Following this lead, James Prothro and Charles Grigg examine the nature of the proposition, often alluded to but never before thoroughly examined, that democracy demands widespread agreement about basic norms of political conduct, especially in terms of minority rights. At the very broad level there is a consensus, they argue, that in abstract terms can be described as a commitment to democracy. The principles of majority rule and minority rights seem embedded in American culture to the extent that there is almost unanimity in responses supporting these abstractions. On the other hand, there is little consensus over specific applications of these community norms. Prothro and Grigg conclude that democracy does not necessarily need broad-based consensual agreement on fundamental norms. What protects democratic norms is apathy. The fact that there is a difference between what people say and what people do, they continue, may account for the persistence of democratic norms even though agreement on specifics is limited. "Discussions of consensus tend to overlook the functional nature of apathy for the democratic system. No one is surprised to hear that what people say they *believe* and what they *actually do* are not necessarily the same. . . . But something close to the opposite may be true: many people express undemocratic principles in response to questioning but are too apathetic to act on their undemocratic opinions in concrete situations. And in most cases, fortunately for the democratic system, those with the most undemocratic principles are also those who are least likely to act." [28]

Prothro and Grigg go on to say that the leadership strata, as "carriers of the creed," behave democratically almost by habit, because of their education and training. Although this is presented as a conclusion, there is no evidence to support the idea that leaders do in fact behave democratically. It might be that as with nonleaders, there is a difference between what leaders say and what they do.

The "habitual democratic behavior" of the leadership elements cannot be taken as a given without thorough examination of whether or not these leadership norms are reflected in the behavior of leaders in actual situations. On the contrary, instances such as Watergate may suggest that leaders often use institutional power in ways that are not tolerant or democratic.

Perhaps the most definitive statement in the literature is the article by Herbert McClosky on ideology and consensus. Political influentials, he says, "manifest by comparison with ordinary voters a more developed sense of ideology and a firmer grasp of the essentials [of democracy]." [29] He supports the work of Prothro and Grigg in finding that influentials have

a more coherent and ordered set of beliefs than the average
citizen. They are "carriers of the creed" responsible for maintaining democratic institutions.

Ultimately McClosky suggests that the widespread abstractions others call the procedural rules are given substance because of a shared consensus among leaders. The passivity of
the ordinary person is the result of "ignorance" and "indiffer-
ence," and he is not likely to do much harm. Here McClosky is
talking about protecting democracy from the people. The political stratum—the articulate, upper-class, educated, and influential sector of the community—is the appropriate group to guide
democracy because its commitment to liberal democratic values
is more consistent, coherent, conscious, and meaningful. He
later argues that influentials are more rational because their
value system is not a "knee-jerk" response but a conscious commitment to democratic values.

It is not surprising to find that the preceding studies led
Thomas Dye and Harmon Zeigler to conclude:

> It is the irony of democracy in America that elites,
> not masses, are most committed to democratic values.
> Despite a superficial commitment to the symbols of de-
> mocracy, the American people have a surprisingly weak
> commitment to individual liberty, toleration of diversity,
> or freedom of expression for those who would challenge
> the existing order. Social science research reveals that the
> common man is not attached to the causes of liberty,
> fraternity, or equality. On the contrary, support for free
> speech and press, for freedom of dissent, and for equality
> of opportunity for all is associated with high educational
> levels, prestigious occupations, and high social status.
> Authoritarianism is stronger among the working classes in
> America than among the middle and upper classes. De-
> mocracy would not survive if it depended upon support
> for democratic values among the masses in America.[30]

McClosky shows that the general electorate exhibits a high
degree of political futility as compared to political influentials.
He shows that it has a lower commitment to the "rules of the
game" and a lower level of "fairness" than political leaders.

Could it be that this reaction occurs not because members of this group are uneducated or confused, but because they realize that the deck is stacked and that the game being played according to the rules is a game in which the rules provide advantages to leaders?

On the whole, the major studies discussed so far seem to indicate that political leaders in America are considered carriers and protectors of democratic culture. Leaders are said to play a role functional to democratic values by acting as brokers and intercessors in the game of influence to determine public policy, and they are said to be committed to democratic values. The prevailing image is that politics American style is essentially an open system of political competition in which bargaining and compromise express the major democratic virtue of tolerance. In sum, politics in the American setting is democratic, with power controlled for functional purposes by experts committed to democracy.

The name of the game is influence, and it is played by the professional uniquely equipped to protect our democratic heritage. There is little discussion of the psychopathology or "hidden destructiveness" Lasswell suggests is implicit in politics. Politics, as it is described, is essentially a spectator sport. But the question might be asked, Could it be that some players are lions and others Christians? Underneath the surface a less democratic form of political activity may take place.

Robert Paul Wolff deserves attention when he suggests: "It is as though an umpire were to come upon a baseball game in progress between the big boys and the little boys in which the big boys cheated, broke the rules, claimed hits that were outs, and made the little boys accept the injustice by brute force." [31] If in this situation a researcher asked the big boys if they thought the rules should be obeyed, if the values of the game were beneficial to all concerned, and if they believed violence and coercion have no place in the game, he would get an affirmative response. If, on the other hand, he asked the little boys if they agreed with the rules of the game, if the values of the game were beneficial to all, and if they believed that power and sanctions were inherent in the game, we might find that the little boys are not very good players because they do not think the rules are equitable. We might find that the big boys are open, tolerant, and concerned that the rules be maintained because they do not feel threatened by their application; at the same time, the little boys might feel cheated— that no matter what they do the same people seem to run things—and they might feel a little cynical about participating, so that they choose to watch rather than play. In this conclusion we might miss the actual power relationship that the abstractly "fair" rules obscure.

The following quotation states the argument differently:

> Procedural democracy [and its view of democratic professionals committed to liberal democracy] defines justice as equal treatment for all regardless of the particular situation. Since there is no justifiable basis for distinguishing differences of race, black men should receive the same treatment as white men. But this means that black men, being now at a disadvantage, will retain that disadvantage.
>
> The so-called neutral rules applied equally to all perpetuate the inequality; from the perspective of the non-legitimate [apolitical] groups such laws are not neutral. They are defined as neutral only by the legitimate groups who use "neutral" laws to protect their existing positions.[32]

If this is akin to the situation in American politics, it would not be surprising to find that the influential would agree that the rules should be applied in an egalitarian way, including specific concrete situations pertaining to free speech, press, or assembly. It would also not be surprising that noninfluentials do not overwhelmingly support the application of democratic norms. It might be possible to think of democratic rules and procedures as something other than expressions of enlightened community leaders. Experts in politics (i.e., the best game-players) may also be the most skillful in using the rules to maintain the game that gives them an advantage. In other words, applying the rules universally may ultimately have the effect of managing the array of interests in favor of prevailing power-holders within the society.

Images of politics are related to the social, economic, and political contexts that form the bases for perception. The benign image of power which pervades contemporary studies of politics certainly must have an empirical referent in experience. But after the political turmoil of the 1960s and the Watergate scandal of the seventies, can this image of leadership be maintained without modification? If this paper demonstrates little else, it should at least indicate that our image of leadership is problematic.

One critical viewer of the redefined democratic image suggests that recent major changes in higher education have contributed to this supportive view of American democracy:

> How have we gotten into this situation in which the main thrust of . . . speculation is conservative rather than favorable to change? Before World War II, I think it is fair to say, the opposite situation prevailed. What then are the causes of post–World War II conservatism? In the first place, there was the usual let-down from the idealism generated during the war to sustain the struggle. In the second place, the cold war brought about a strong anticommunist reaction from American liberals which took the form of an idealization of the American status quo. The heightening of anticommunist hysteria after the fall of China and Czechoslovakia brought with it McCarthyism and fear among hitherto liberal intellectuals. Furthermore, the enlistment of academics in the cold war contributed an additional set of rationalizations to the conservative position. Another factor which may have influenced the trend was the steady decline of alienation among academic intellectuals. In contrast to the situation in the thirties, there have been plenty of jobs since the war and jobs open to all. The decline of discrimination in academic employment has been a distinctive feature of the postwar situation.[33]

It is possible to add other speculations about the causes of the new images constructed in academia but perhaps it is not worthwhile to do so here. The question is, What is to be done now that recent political events challenge comfortable conceptions of American democracy?

One thing that might happen, and has happened too often in the past, is that scholars can ignore anomalous new data and reify their theories. Or scholars might "kill the messenger" —that is, criticize the media, the dissidents, and other scapegoats as somehow responsible. Or researchers might reassert the critical idea of democracy and search for the "hidden destructiveness of our cultural institutions." If the third alternative is pursued, then Barrington Moore offers a useful suggestion. "For all students of human society, sympathy with the victims of historical processes and skepticism about the visitors' claims provide essential safeguards against being taken in by the dominant mythology. A scholar who tries to be objective needs these feelings as part of his ordinary working equipment." [34]

That critical edge Moore supports might be developed by rethinking the prevailing view of political power and leadership. Whether traditional democracy provides that ingredient is not the conclusion of this article. It is clear that suspicion of power, regardless of the purpose for which it is rationalized, is part of the American heritage. On this point at least, recent political experience can teach us something of great value: never presume that political leadership in American society will protect or defend democratic values. Americans must do it themselves.

NOTES

1. Harold D. Lasswell, *Power and Personality* (New York: Viking Press, 1948), pp. 10–12.

2. Ibid., p. 38. An important point to note here for later discussion is that Lasswell suggests that political leaders who accentuate power will always "rationalize" that use of power in terms of the general good.

3. Ibid., p. 173.

4. For examples of studies that are charged with redefining traditional democratic values, see: Joseph Schumpeter, *Capitalism, Socialism and Democracy* (New York: Harper Publishing Co., 1942); Bernard Berelson, et al., *Voting* (Chicago: University of Chicago Press, 1954); Berelson, "Democratic Theory and Public Opinion," *Public Opinion Quarterly* 16 (Fall 1952): 313–30; Gabriel Almond and Sidney Verba, *Civic Culture* (Boston: Little, Brown and Co., 1962); and especially Robert Dahl, *Who Governs?* (New Haven,

Conn.: Yale University Press, 1961). Making the charges are a number of authors including Peter Bachrach, *The Theory of Democratic Elitism: A Critique* (Boston: Little, Brown and Co., 1967); Graeme Duncan and Stephen Lukes, "The New Democracy," *Political Studies* 11 (1963): 156–77; Jack L. Walker, "A Critique of the Elitist Theory of Democracy," *The American Political Science Review* 60 (June 1966), pp. 285–95; and Maure L. Goldschmidt, "Democratic Theory and Contemporary Political Science," *Western Political Quarterly* 19, no. 3, Supplement (1966). Many of these articles as well as others are collected and reprinted in Charles McCoy and John Playford, *Apolitical Politics: A Critique of Behavioralism* (New York: Thoms Y. Crowell Co., 1967).

5. For a good review of the literature on procedural democracy, see David Ricci, *Community Power and Democratic Theory: The Logic of Political Analysis* (New York: Random House, 1971), pp. 50–64. It is not possible to explore here all of the potential theories dealing with the role of political leaders. Very broadly we can say that many of the classical theories concerning the role of leaders stressed them as the articulators, protectors, and most able representatives of dominant class values. Democratic leaders on the other hand, are presumed to provide a service as representatives of various values in a multivalued (or secularized) society. The most classic definitive statement of ruling-class theory is provided by Gaetano Mosca, *The Ruling Class,* trans. Hannah D. Kahn (New York: McGraw-Hill, 1939). Democracy for Mosca was essentially a facade in which the ruling class maintained its power, and representative government was different in practice from the expressed democratic ideals.

6. Ricci, *Community Power,* p. 51.

7. For example, see Charles F. Cnudde and Dean E. Neubauer, eds., *Empirical Democratic Theory* (Chicago: Markham Publishing Co., 1969) which includes a series of writings that are "descriptive" of democratic culture and processes. For a critical evaluation of much of the literature on process democracy see George D. Beam, *Usual Politics* (New York: Holt, Rinehart and Winston, 1970), pp. 119–22.

8. Anthony Downs, *An Economic Theory of Democracy* (New York: Harper and Brothers, 1957), pp. 20–21.

9. Beam, *Usual Politics,* p. 111.

10. Almond and Verba, *Civic Culture,* p. 343.

11. The concept of balance is important here in Almond and Verba (p. 354), because the civic culture demands that extremes

be avoided in participation. Thus a primary concern is giving elites the necessary power to be able to achieve functional goals. An evaluation and critique of balance and the concept of equilibrium can be found in Beam, *Usual Politics,* pp. 95–108. The presumption seems to be that participation must be permitted, but limited, in order that elites may behave responsibly. Limited participation means electoral participation, but the question of whether or not this is effective participation goes largely unanswered.

12. Almond and Verba, *Civic Culture,* p. 340.

13. Gabriel A. Almond, "Comparative Political Systems," *Journal of Politics* 18 (August 1956): 391–409.

14. Richard E. Neustadt, *Presidential Power* (New York: John Wiley & Sons, 1960), p. 19.

15. Henry S. Kariel, *The Promise of Politics* (Englewood Cliffs, N.J.: Prentice-Hall, 1966), pp. 112–13. This point about permanent political defeat is made quite forcefully by Kariel when he says: "The available studies [pluralist process studies] take no account of the fact that children who lost out because of a legislative compromise on an education bill have lost out forever, that citizens evacuated, aliens deported, workers never employed at all or never employed at their potential capacity, men and women never cured or rehabilitated or treated have heard the last word. For them decisions are irrevocable. Their defeats are final." Perhaps some might expect a different view of the political process from below rather than the prevailing one presented from above.

16. Donald R. Mathews, *U.S. Senators and Their World* (New York: Random House, 1960).

17. Ibid., p. 45.

18. Karl Mannheim, *Man and Society in an Age of Reconstruction* (New York: Harcourt, Brace & World, 1940), pp. 55, 58–59.

19. William Kornhauser, *The Politics of Mass Society* (New York: Free Press of Glencoe, 1959).

20. Ibid., pp. 229, 233. Neither Mannheim nor Kornhauser suggests that a fundamental alteration of the social structure, especially from the Left, would mitigate the pathology of mass industrial society as they see it. Kornhauser is explicitly concerned with the preservation of an environment that will foster democratic elites, rather than an environment that will foster democratic participation on a society-wide scale. Again this is expressive of the presumption in many studies that mass participation carries with it irrational forms of political behavior.

21. Giuseppe Di Palma, *Apathy and Participation: Mass Politics*

in Western Societies (New York: Free Press of Glencoe, 1970), p. 4.

22. Ibid., p. 3.
23. Dahl, *Who Governs?*, p. 307.
24. Ibid., pp. 316, 317.
25. Ibid., p. 363.
26. Ibid., p. 306. As spectators, or in Dahl's phrase through "citizenship without politics," the institutions perform their role of mobilizing resources, coordinating activities, recruiting experts or professionals with these skills, and providing spectator entertainment. It was essentially this point that made Walker wonder if the black populations in New Haven that rioted a few years after Dahl's study were enjoying the game.
27. Samuel A. Stouffer, *Communism, Conformity, and Civil Liberties* (New York: Doubleday & Co., 1955).
28. James W. Prothro and Charles M. Grigg, "Fundamental Principles of Democracy: Bases of Agreement and Disagreement," *American Political Science Review* 22 (1960): 293.
29. Herbert McClosky, "Consensus and Ideology in American Politics," *American Political Science Review* 58 (1964): 362.
30. Thomas R. Dye and L. Harmon Zeigler, *The Irony of Democracy*, 2d ed. (N. Scituate, Mass.: Duxbury Press, 1971), p. 18.
31. Robert Paul Wolff, *The Poverty of Liberalism* (Boston: Beacon Press, 1968), p. 157.
32. Beam, *Usual Politics*, p. 121.
33. Maure L. Goldschmidt, "Democratic Theory and Contemporary Political Science," pp. 6–7.
34. Barrington Moore, Jr., *Social Origins of Dictatorship and Democracy* (Boston: Beacon Press, 1966), p. 523.

Amnesty and Fairness:
The Power to Educate and
the Duty to Dissent

GLEN STASSEN

Usually when we think of "power and education" we think of something fairly tame and academic. But during the past decade, the major meeting place between power and education was the Vietnam war and the discussion it created. The war was education, in the sense that no other event in the past decade taught the nation more or changed its way of thinking more. And the war was power, the power of killing and death, and the political power of the struggle to change minds and policies about the war's continuation.

Many of those who sought to develop a widespread popular protest powerful enough to stop the war were students from our nation's educational institutions. Furthermore, colleges, universities, and high schools were a major source of young men confronted by the power of the state to draft and to force a decision whether to fight or not. A significant part of the educational process was the highly motivated discussion of the war, what to do about the war, and what to do about the draft call. By contrast with their counterparts of the fifties, students in the sixties were more engaged with questions of values, ethics, and social purpose. Discussion of the war and the draft made a significant difference in the lives of students, in the life of the nation, and in the educational process.

And the education is still going on. I cite a letter from Walter Davis, a student in the college where I taught:

In 1967, I joined the Peace Corps and served two years in Colombia as an agricultural and community development volunteer, attached to the Colombian land reform agency. Before Peace Corps, I had worked part time in remedial reading in volunteer work with the Appalachian Volunteers (VISTA), as well as being a student president of a small Baptist college (Kentucky Southern), a church youth leader and a full time youth organizer with the Democratic Party in the spring of 1967.

I tell you all that not to elicit sympathy, but to point out that I was the average active young American torn loose by the war in Vietnam; and because in 1969, when I returned from the Peace Corps, . . . I received an induction notice.

I appealed on the basis that I was a conscientious objector whose entire life and religious beliefs and present conscience made it impossible for me to kill another human being or in any way to be a party to bloodshed. . . . A religiously biased draft board ruled that since my church (Southern Baptist) supported killing in "Just Wars," my personal objection was invalid. . . . No testimony was allowed, nor was legal counsel; and, in fact, no appeal hearing was granted. . . . Thus, every particle of due process was denied to me.

I came to Canada in 1969 and was cleared as a landed immigrant in 1970. The religious prejudice of my local draft board had forced me to choose to select either *induction* which was morally repugnant to me, *imprisonment* which I felt could not contribute anything to the world or my own well-being, or *exile*.

In 1970, I learned that the Supreme Court ruled that conscientious objection was a matter of personal moral beliefs and not primarily tied to religious affiliation or practice. Nonetheless, the Selective Service in Kentucky took me and nine other draft resisters (who were all strangely enough exemplary in one way or another as student leaders, sons of outstanding pacifists, etc.) to trial in absentia. We were indicted, having almost all been denied the minimum of due process . . . , access to the charges and evidence against us as well as [notification] of the charges and hearing—no difficulty in my case, since my local board received regular notice of my change of address.

I contend that all the charges and decisions of the Selective Service against me were unconstitutional from the outset.

Walter Davis raises a question that anyone interested in power and education ought to think through with care. By now most of us have probably come to conclusions similar to his concerning the war, though some of us probably have not. But we all recognize various kinds of dissent, including his thought and action, as one inevitable result of education, if education is not merely memorization and recall. Education, when it is healthy, teaches people to think more deeply, to value truth, to take that truth seriously as they act. Walter was acting upon what he had come to think and value when he decided to join the Peace Corps, and then to resist the war in Vietnam. His action was part of a long tradition of reform and dissent that emerges periodically from disciples of prophets and philosophers, from the monks of a Cluny monastery or a Franciscan order, and from the college, seminary, or university. Without that long tradition of dissent, education would resemble a mere tracing of shadows rather than an existential groping toward the light.

The obligation to dissent when truth points in the direction of dissent is an inherent requirement of truthful education. The result is sometimes confrontation between education and power. Sometimes it leads to conscientious refusal to obey a law such as the draft law. In this sense, Walter Davis was typical of hundreds of thousands who entered the fray without either skilled legal counsel or legally prescribed due process. In 1963–1964, about 45 percent of those who applied for status as conscientious objectors obtained it. In 1965, the figure dropped to 25 percent, and from 1966 on, only 4 percent were granted their requests for conscientious objector status.[1] This striking nationwide shift in the judgments of draft boards coincided with the decision of the administration to send massive numbers of soldiers to Vietnam. The shift seems to have been caused by the desire to fill quotas rather than by a sudden drop in the quality of C.O. applications.

For those of us concerned about power and education, regardless of our views concerning wars, that war, and the draft, the protest against the war represents the inevitable progeny of our efforts and our concerns. It represents searching for truth, without censoring truth which disagrees with the policies of governmental authorities, and acting upon that truth, without flinching when it results in conflict with power. The resisters are our progeny; how can we not think long and hard about our responsibility for the issues they raise?

The issue is not yet behind us, for several reasons. The basic questions of what is fair in dealing with those who resist a war and disobey a law or an order will probably arise again. What we learn from the Vietnam experience will influence what we do in the future. Of more immediate concern, there are perhaps 30,000 deserters at large, 792,500 veterans with less-than-honorable discharges, and 100,000 to 200,000 civilians who were arrested for antiwar activity.[2] Amnesty in the United States, especially after divisive wars, has historically come in stages of increasing inclusiveness as new presidents took office. For offenders in the Civil War, President Lincoln proclaimed two amnesties, Andrew Johnson four, and Congress several, making it almost universal in 1872 and truly universal in 1898. After World War I, President Wilson pardoned a few, Coolidge a few more, and finally in 1933 President Roosevelt granted universal amnesty to all draft resisters. There is no reason to expect that the pattern after the Vietnam war will be different. Presidents Ford's and Carter's partial answers may be only the first stages. The issue is still with us.

Since this is so, I want to raise a question of fairness that is curiously bypassed in the literature. And I want to raise it not from the perspective of the partisan who already knows the answer but from the perspective of one who searches for a reasoned way to address questions of fairness.

The issue of fairness is an intriguing one in the amnesty discussion. On the one hand, Walter Davis's letter quoted above is permeated by questions about fairness and arguments that appeal to fairness from the first sentence to the last. He is asking what is the fair way to treat draft resisters. His arguments are not answered by those who oppose amnesty; they are bypassed. On the other hand, the argument against amnesty I hear most frequently is that amnesty would not be fair to those who died in Vietnam. This is the main argument presented by John P. Martha in his article in the *American Legion*.[3] Martha points out the tragic price paid for the Vietnam struggle by Americans: 1,800,000 Americans were drafted, 46,226 died, 303,654 were wounded, 772 captured, and 1,088 are missing in action. Amnesty for those who did not serve would be unfair to those who did.

It is an odd characteristic of the literature on amnesty that the question of fairness is not well answered. It is usually rejected as the wrong question—and usually for good reasons, I admit. But I cannot reject the question completely, and because it keeps being raised by those who have doubts about amnesty, and by many plain folk who have not read the literature on amnesty, I suspect that either the question is an important one or that something important is hidden within it or underneath it.

Julian C. Carey, in the *Saint Louis University Law Journal*, argues cogently that "the issue of amnesty toward these men does not lend itself to a balancing of equities between those who served and those who refused. Does the grief of a family who lost a loved one in Indochina diminish if another family realizes that their loved one can never return to the United States? Is the soldier who was wounded and permanently disabled in Indochina made whole if another man is tried, convicted, and incarcerated for refusing to serve?"[4] The absurdity of trying to equalize the suffering is obvious, because there is no way to equalize it, and doing so would do no good. Young men died, and others were permanently disabled in Vietnam; no one proposes that a group of resisters should be chosen for an equal fate. Even those who speak—loosely, I think—of equalizing the penalty are somewhat aware that there is a vindictive sound to their words. Thus Ernest van den Haag writes that he "would want to make sure" that the resister "did not get any advantage from his evasion of the draft, that he is in no way better off. . . . But . . . *I would not want to be vindictive. On the other hand* . . . I would indeed assert the law in its full gravity. Any time that he returns to the United States unrepentant, I would certainly want to inflict that punishment on him that the law provides." [5]

Anyone who knows the experience of receiving the visit from the officer who tells you that your own father or son or husband or brother was killed in action knows it is absurd to speak of "not getting any advantage from his evasion of the draft." And knows too that vindictiveness does not help; it can dissolve your soul in resentment. The question of fairness cannot be the question of equalizing the suffering.

There is another reason why putting the question this way is wrong. It aims at the wrong target. Thus Martin Marty points out that the exiles and deserters have already suffered in a way those who avoided the draft legally did not: "Were I in a family where someone had been lost in Vietnam, I would be much more resentful of the affluent sons of senators and representatives and university professors who were able, certainly before any draft laws changed, to get exemptions and to get by without any kind of inconvenience. Remember that most young people were not in any way inconvenienced by Vietnam. The exile was . . . the subject of suspicion overseas; he left behind a girl-friend, brothers, sisters, parents, friends." [6]

More pertinent is the fact that many of us shared the exile's belief that the war was immoral, unjust, and illegal. I ask myself how much suffering I underwent to stop the war and get the soldiers home before they were killed. If I believed as the exiles did, and differed only in that I was older and had a family, why did I not act on my beliefs to share in the loss experienced by those who went to Vietnam and those who went to Canada? Insofar as we take seriously our responsibilities as citizens of this nation, and want to advance the claim of equity or fairness, I think this is the question we must ask.

The question of equity and fairness can also be used to criticize the government. William Wick argues that "to attempt to equalize the suffering by heaping more 'unfairness' on those who refused to go is only a shallow, pitiful effort by the government to evade its own singular responsibility for Vietnam and its awful consequences." John Swomley describes it as "the familiar device of pitting one group of victims against another in order to deny justice to both." Government leaders did not suffer forced exile; yet it was they who made the decisions that led to the suffering of Vietnamese and Americans. The resisters, on the other hand, "suffered imprisonment, exile, loss of jobs or other penalties, but they did contribute to decisions to bring ground troops home from Vietnam and hence to the lowering of casualties." And James Childress points out that "there is no way we can repay those persons who suffered and died in Vietnam . . . by punishing those who opposed the war and fled." Instead we should insist that the government turn its attention to helping veterans find jobs and the injured find better treatment. If instead we concentrate on the fairness question, "we may use punishment and even conditional amnesty as an excuse for failing to do as much as we should for all the victims of this war and for failing to attend to the serious wounds in the nation as a whole." [7]

All these arguments agree that if fairness means everyone should bear the suffering equally, then fairness in war cannot be achieved. Some were killed in Vietnam; others stayed home and protested or supported the war quietly and in comfort. The exiles suffered less than those who were killed or wounded and more than the rest of us who stayed home. There is no way to equalize that.

That is why presidents, from Washington, Adams, Jefferson, and Madison through Lincoln, Johnson, Roosevelt, Ford, and Carter, have all granted amnesty not in the name of fairness, but in the name of peace and the public good and the need to bind up the wounds of the people, to heal the nation, to "lull strife to sleep," to put enmity behind us, and to seek a new beginning. They felt it was consistent with their own morality, and with the purpose of this nation of refugees and immigrants, to express, once the war was over, a degree of mercy, pardon, forgiveness, or generosity. Hence Charles Lutz, writing in the *Christian Century*, states that if amnesty is granted, "the idea of fairness will suffer. Amnesty does not put a high value on fairness; neither does grace." [8] He then comes down on the side of amnesty because of his loyalty to grace, mercy, and the Scriptures.

So those who still oppose amnesty argue in the name of fairness, and those who favor it argue on the grounds of healing, mercy, the common good, and tradition, and on the ground that this war was wrong and the resisters were right. The arguments go past each other.

Is the fairness question totally irrelevant? Or does its persistence suggest it has valid content which deserves a more concerted answer? We have seen that it is an impossible question if it means that people should suffer equally. But there are at least three other meanings that opponents have in mind, and that need to be considered. First, we had the draft because we believed some day the nation might need to fight a war that *is* justified. Is it fair for some to answer the draft while others choose not to? Second, citizenship involves a duty to one's country. Is it not fair that resisters do some act such as alternative service in order to express their political obligation? Third, resisters violated the law. Is it not fair that there be some penalty? What penalty *is* fair?

The difficulty with these questions is that for some they are so forceful as to be conclusive and almost impossible to answer in the negative, while for others they are so patently false, especially in the context of the Vietnam war, that they should not be taken seriously. The questions engage loyalties and passions concerning the nature of this war and other wars, the character of recent presidents and their war decisions, and the obligation to obey the law or to oppose unjust law. In an issue of this sort, is there a way to think through what is fair?

No other book on ethics within living memory has received the attention that John Rawls's A *Theory of Justice* is receiving.[9] Furthermore, Rawls bases his work on the principle of fairness— the focus of our question. The book is notable in its urging that ethical principles be tested by how they work out in particular cases—and in its own faithfulness to that admonition. Hence it has particular promise for our question about fairness in the case of amnesty.

Rawls begins by defining conditions under which we say a

decision is fair. If all those affected by a decision are free to disagree, are rational, and have an equal voice in the decision, and they all reach agreement on the decision, we say their decision is fair. So Rawls says that "the guiding idea is that the principles of justice for the basic structure of society (if they are fair) . . . are the principles that free and rational persons concerned to further their own interests would accept in an initial position of equality. This way of regarding the principles of justice I shall call justice as fairness." [10]

An obvious source of unfairness is that people are biased in favor of their own interests and ideologies and that they allow these biases to influence decisions. The judge who has accepted a bribe, the juror who is racially prejudiced, the president who depends on contributions from a wealthy interest group, the member of the Agriculture Committee who stands to receive large subsidies from the legislation that he votes upon, all are likely to make decisions that are not fair, because the decisions will be biased in favor of their own interests and values. So Rawls asks us to imagine we are in a hypothetical situation, behind a "veil of ignorance":

> Among the essential features of this situation is that no one knows his place in society, his class position or social status, nor does any one know his fortune in the distribution of natural assets and abilities, his intelligence, strength, and the like. I shall even assume that the parties do not know their conceptions of the good or their special psychological propensities. The principles of justice are chosen behind a veil of ignorance. This ensures that no one is advantaged or disadvantaged in the choice of principles by the outcome of natural chance or the contingency of social circumstances. [11]

Suppose two brothers love lemon pie and need to divide a piece with one small strawberry on it. The one with the power to cut the pie is likely to rationalize that the strawberry should be on his half because he appreciates strawberries more than his brother does. His brother, likewise viewing the division with biased eyes, will argue that the strawberry is worth at least two tablespoons of pie, and that in any case his brother's piece is bigger than his. The fair solution which has occurred to many a hassled parent is the "pie principle." The brother who cuts the pie cuts it from behind the veil of ignorance. He does not know which piece of pie will be his and which will be his brother's. After he has cut the pie, the pieces may be distributed by the throw of dice. Or his brother may be given the choice of pieces. The one who does the cutting will try to achieve an objectively fair division because he does not know which piece he will end up with.

This strikes us as fair. How would it apply to the amnesty question? If we place ourselves behind the veil of ignorance, we must imagine the situation of the young man (or soon, perhaps, the young woman) who has just received a draft call to fight a war. But for the moment we must rule out our knowledge or our moral convictions concerning the war and the draft. I may be a person who believes firmly that this particular war violates major principles of a just war, and neither five years in prison nor a lifetime of exile would induce me to betray the long-standing teachings of the church, the principles of justice for which my nation stands, and my own conscience. Or I may be a person who believes firmly that a citizen must obey his or her government, and neither a year in Vietnam nor the chance of being killed or wounded would induce me to betray the long history of my country, its laws, and my own sense of patriotism. From behind the veil of ignorance, imagining that I might enter society with either set of convictions, how could I decide what is a fair penalty for rejecting the draft call and going into exile?

I must try to choose a penalty that will be in my interest, assuming that in real life I might become either a conscientious resister or a conscientious supporter of this war and of the draft. What penalty will I choose?

Consider the interests of the conscientious supporter of the war and the draft. His main concern is for national security or the defense of the country. William Rusher, for example, is worried that amnesty would encourage desertion and draft evasion in future wars. He argues that drafted manpower is essential to the state's military strength. Therefore anyone "who, by dodging the draft or deserting the armed forces, arbitrarily removes himself from that manpower pool, is striking directly at the state's ability to implement its policies—perhaps, even to survive." [12]

If it is difficult to hide behind the veil of ignorance and imagine ourselves in Rusher's shoes, it may help to conjure up memories of World War II or a hypothetical war that we would consider justified. If a dictator should arise who intends to conquer the world, to remove our freedoms and those of everyone else, including the freedom to be a conscientious war resister, and to exterminate a race of people who number in the millions, we want him stopped. If he has the power to succeed unless our nation completely mobilizes, and if complete mobilization is likely to defeat him in conventional war (an important new "if," since the nuclear bomb) with a smaller number of deaths than would occur if we do not fight, then most of us will probably concede the need for a draft, and for its being obeyed. (This may be difficult for some, but we are to stay behind the veil of ignorance for the time being.) Under such conditions, we would want those drafted to have a strong incentive to accept the call.

The argument here is a special application of Rawls's argument for the natural duty of justice. "The most important natural duty is that to support and to further just institutions. This duty has two parts: first, we are to comply with and to do our share in just institutions when they exist and apply to us; and second, we are to assist in the establishment of just arrangements when they do not exist, at least when this can be done with little cost to ourselves." [13] Although Rawls does not elaborate, the cost we would be willing to expend would depend on the importance of the institution. From the veil of ignorance, we might consider the institution of forming orderly lines at movie theaters a just institution, but we would not define the natural duty to support that institution as worth the cost of a life or even a close friendship; a harsh glance, however, or a word of censure, might be an appropriate cost. On the other hand, to support the basic freedoms of the society against being overwhelmed by a malevolent dictator, we would set the worthwhile cost higher.

The reason why the natural duty of justice is fair is that

in the original position (that is, from behind the veil of ignorance), we would want that duty to exist. We would know that "from a self-interested point of view each person is tempted to shirk doing his share. He benefits from the public good in any case." Furthermore, since "compliance with a cooperative venture is predicated on the belief that others will do their part, citizens may be tempted to avoid making a contribution when they believe, or with reason suspect, that others are not making theirs." The result is that without a natural duty of justice, private self-interest might dissolve those cooperative ventures that all from behind the veil of ignorance would agree is in their mutual interest. "Therefore the parties in the original position do best when they acknowledge that natural duty of justice." [14]

A major concern of fairness for those who oppose amnesty is that a significant number of citizens might for selfish reasons shirk their duty to fight in a just war. This might result in the disintegration of the war effort, and in unfairness to those who do accept the draft call. If those who favor amnesty can imagine conscientious persons believing the degree of truth in this argument, it can help heal some bitterness the war has left us. The argument has particular force for those who, when they think of war and the draft, think of World War II.

But the argument depends on the war's being one we would conscientiously support, or on our imagining ourselves holding Rusher's beliefs. Now suppose we imagine ourselves holding the beliefs of a draft resister. Even though this is difficult for some, it may help to focus on the Vietnam war, or one even more unjustified. Let us imagine that the purpose of the war is to support a dictator who would have been rejected by his own country if he had not canceled the elections he had promised to hold; that participation in the war is contrary to the wishes of the people of the United States; that it may take eight years and two presidential elections before we can get out of the war; and that, in the meantime, if we continue to prosecute the war, several million human beings, mostly civilians, will be killed. Suppose the war is unconstitutional and usual democratic processes for stopping American involvement have been tried but are subverted by governmental deception and by the use of various branches of government to undermine dissent. Suppose that if everyone who is drafted goes to fight, the war may last ten years, but if half of them refuse, forces will coalesce against the war, its duration will be cut in half, and three million lives will be saved.

In this hypothetical war, what would we want the penalty for draft resistance to be? Again, we must imagine ourselves behind the veil of ignorance, not knowing what general convictions we might have about the justification of wars or drafts or penalties in general. We are considering only this case, in which we believe the war to be unconscionably evil and the draft its instrument. In this case, most of us would concede that it would be better if people would reject the draft call in large numbers. Under these conditions we would want those drafted to have a low incentive to accept the call, or better yet, an incentive to reject the call. We would want people to reject the draft in massive numbers, for conscientious reasons or selfish reasons or any reasons.

If this case is not persuasive, then I ask the reader to imagine his or her own case, with the durations and deaths multiplied, the president an insane dictator, his lock on the decision-making apparatus even stronger. One might imagine Hitler's Germany, and ask what incentives for German citizens to obey the draft call would be most conducive to justice. Surely a conclusion is emerging. We would all want greater incentives to obey a draft call when it is just and prudent for our nation to fight a war, and lesser incentives to obey the call when the war is unjust. At some point on the scale of injustice, we would all want a war to be opposed and would want positive incentives for draftees to check the government and turn it around.

This conclusion applies the same natural duty of justice discussed above. The natural duty of justice is to support and to further just institutions. We are to assist in the establishment of just arrangements when they do not exist. In our hypothetical unjust war, the war is unjust, and the just arrangements we have a duty to help establish are in fact those that work to terminate the war.

Something like this concern about the duty to oppose an unjust war underlies the sense of fairness as argued by proponents of amnesty. Martin Marty believes it is good that perhaps "we are past the days of simplicity, of 'my country right or wrong,' of in-

volvement on any terms that we might like, in any kind of war."
Peter Steinfels argues the need for resistance as a check against
wars that are unjust and that lack support from the people. He
points out that "foreign policy is an area that has nearly become
exempt from the principle of checks and balances." And Arthur
Egendorf puts it more pointedly: "Hopefully, more people will
come to realize that unquestioned deference to higher authorities
has been a self-serving cop-out. . . . We have delegated responsibility for the life and death of millions to men who gained power
through unrelenting attention to their own self-interest, with the
delusionary expectation that once in office, they would act with
the wisdom of philosophers. The most perceptive and sensitive
individuals can be trapped by a need to preserve their tenure in
office, incapable of correcting mistakes even after they are
recognized." [15]

In sum, while Rusher argues that there may be wars we should
fight, others argue the Vietnam war was a war we clearly should
not have fought. The overwhelming majority of Americans have
now concluded the war was at least a mistake. The war began
because the Saigon regime refused to hold an election it had
promised at Geneva but knew it would lose to Ho Chi Minh; the
war's purpose to keep that regime in power was both morally
wrong and militarily unrealistic in view of the lack of popular
support in Vietnam; its cost in lives and goods and in international
peace was far out of proportion to any likely benefit; its massive
systematic bombing of civilians with fragmentation bombs and
napalm violated morality and the rules of war; it was undeclared
either by constitutional processes in the United States or by the
United Nations; and it was sidled into by systematic deception of
the American people. If another president should be tempted to
engage in a war this unjust again, we would want him or her to
worry that extensive draft resistance might occur again. And if
the nation should be thrust into such a war, we would want
effective resistance to occur early.

We have reached an interesting and somewhat novel conclusion. Fairness would require a large enough penalty to deter
very extensive shirking in a justified war (should one occur), and
small enough not to deter refusal in an unjustified war (should
one occur). This suggests that we would consider it fair to adjust

the penalty according to the degree of justification, which is a novel suggestion and requires further examination. But first, let us examine the nature of conscientious refusal which led us to this conclusion.

Rawls weaves together two arguments for conscientious refusal and confuses them a bit. Disentangling them may be worthwhile. The first argument concerns liberty of conscience. From behind the veil of ignorance, people would not know what their moral or religious convictions are, or whether they are in the majority. "Now it seems that equal liberty of conscience is the only principle that [they] . . . can acknowledge. They cannot take chances with their liberty by permitting the dominant religious or moral doctrine to persecute or to suppress others if it wishes." This argument would apply to questions of conscience on matters of war, since in an age of threatened nuclear war and mass destruction, along with ideological clashes, war becomes a question of strongly held conscientious convictions. Rawls points out that his "idea is to generalize the principle of religious toleration to a social form, thereby arriving at equal liberty in public institutions." And the most fundamental principle of justice his method of fairness establishes is that "each person is to have an equal right to the most extensive basic liberty compatible with a similar liberty for others." [16] The principle is not unlike the equal liberty principle that diverse philosophers in the Western tradition, including both utilitarians and Kantians, have adopted, and it is not likely to be controversial for most readers.

The characteristic feature of Rawls's argument is that it is based solely on the conception of fairness in which people who temporarily do not know their conscientious convictions would protect everyone's liberty of conscience as potentially their own. "Toleration is not derived from practical necessities or reasons of state. Moral and religious freedom follows from the principle of equal liberty; and assuming the priority of this principle, the only ground for denying the equal liberties is to avoid an even greater injustice, and even greater loss of liberty. . . . The limitation of liberty is justified only when it is necessary for liberty itself, to prevent an invasion of freedom that would be still worse." [17]

This argument applies to the question of conscientious refusal. "Conscientious refusal is noncompliance with a more or less direct legal injunction or administrative order." Unlike civil disobedience, which is undertaken as a public appeal based on widely held public or political principles of justice, conscientious refusal may be simply an overt or covert refusal to violate one's own religious or moral conscientious principles. Typical examples of conscientious refusal that Rawls mentions are the refusal of early Christians to worship Roman gods, the refusal of Jehovah's Witnesses to salute the flag, and "the unwillingness of a pacifist to serve in the armed forces, or of a soldier to obey an order that he thinks is manifestly contrary to the moral law as it applies to war." [18] Rawls argues that conscientious refusal of this sort should be tolerated so long as it does not violate the equal liberties of others.

He applies the argument to the draft: "Since conscription is a drastic interference with the basic liberties of equal citizenship, it cannot be justified by any needs less compelling than those of national security." And in defining national security, Rawls explicitly rules out "unjustified foreign adventures," and wars whose objective is "economic advantage or national power." Rather, "Conscription is permissible only if it is demanded for the defense of liberty itself, including here not only the liberties of the citizens of the society in question, but also those of persons in other societies as well." When conscription is for the defense of liberty, then its burdens should be shared in a fair manner by all members of society, and with "no avoidable class bias in selecting those who are called for duty." [19]

With the important exception that the permissible purpose of the draft is defined more precisely, this is Rusher's argument in genteel form. Equal sharing of burdens requires that those who conscientiously refuse the draft be given burdens to share. But this applies only to wars and drafts that defend a liberty greater than the liberty removed by the draft and fighting.

Conscientious refusal may be based on privately held religious or conscientious beliefs, rather than on public principles of justice. The society should tolerate conscientious refusers not because they are right or because they agree with the society's principles, but because of the importance and the fairness of the principle of liberty of conscience.

There are some limits to the helpfulness of this argument for amnesty and war resistance, however. First, because the argument tends to relegate conscientious beliefs to a private or religious realm that is not relevant to public policy, it tends to encourage society to ignore the claim to truth of those beliefs. Society too easily tolerates the right of the beliefs to exist without considering the claim that the war is actually immoral and unjust. At the same time, the government should regulate conscientious refusal when it infringes on equal liberty for all. Hence some argue conscientious refusal to fight a war in defense of liberty may threaten the liberty of others, and should not be tolerated. Furthermore, toleration depends on the sincerity of the conscientious convictions that motivate resisters. Hence some want to limit amnesty to those whose resistance was deeply conscientious, and to grant amnesty only after a case-by-case procedure for testing motives. Opponents of amnesty for deserters argue they deserted for other motives besides conscientious resistance. This fosters the class discrimination of pardoning college students who resisted the draft for articulate conscientious reasons while not pardoning the less-sophisticated working-class men who answered the draft and deserted later for a variety of motives. Finally, toleration requires that those who refuse to fight be given compensatory burdens to share, for the sake of fairness and for the sake of discouraging mere shirking of duty for less than conscientious reasons.

Rawls makes another argument for conscientious refusal, this second argument depending not on toleration and the liberty of conscience, but on the natural duty of justice. We recall Rawls's explanation that we would consider it fair for everyone to have a duty to help establish just arrangements when they do not exist. This means that when war is more an instrument of injustice than justice, there is a natural duty to oppose it and to help establish more just alternatives. "And given the tendency of nations, particularly great powers, to engage in war unjustifiably and to set in motion the apparatus of the state to suppress dissent, the respect accorded to pacifism serves the purpose of alerting citizens to the wrongs that governments are prone to commit in their name." [20]

If we imagine ourselves once again behind the veil of ignorance, representing different nations but not knowing which ones, we would not favor declarations of war merely because we had a loyalty to one nation rather than another. That would be biased and unfair and would be ruled out by the veil of ignorance. Instead, Rawls argues, we would adopt the principles of just-war theory. Rawls refers to writings of Ralph Potter and Paul Ramsey and mentions briefly a few principles we would adopt. A just war must be fought in self-defense, must be consistent with the principle of self-determination, must have as its aim a just peace, and must be fought with just means. There are other principles implied in the characterization of the Vietnam war above, and for which the reader is referred to Potter's *War and Moral Discourse.*[21] These principles are on the one hand held by many leading figures in the history of major Catholic and Protestant denominations and are on the other hand public principles of justice and fairness that would be adopted by rational persons behind the veil of ignorance. Therefore they are neither merely private and "self-appointed," nor claims to a private right or a liberty of conscience. They are not permissions, but obligations, duties—natural duties which obligate every person. "Therefore if a soldier is ordered to engage in certain illicit acts of war, he may [Rawls should say *has a duty to*] refuse if he reasonably and conscientiously believes that the principles applying to the conduct of war are plainly violated. He can [*ought to*] maintain that all things considered, his natural duty not to be made the agent of grave injustice and evil to another outweighs his duty to obey." [22] Rawls's argument is clear: he describes the natural duty each of us has to establish justice and resist injustice. Only because his argument is mixed with the earlier argument about toleration of equal liberty does he slip into the language of toleration or permission, using "may" and "can."

It is clear that under conditions of fairness, behind the veil of ignorance, we would want citizens of a nation beginning to engage in prosecuting an unjust war to resist their government's decision to make war. We would want that to be a duty and not merely a tolerated right. In that case, as Rawls concludes, "A person may [ought to] conscientiously refuse to comply with his duty to enter the armed forces during a particular war on the grounds that the aims of the conflict are unjust. . . . A citizen may [ought to] maintain that once it is clear that the moral law of war is being regularly violated, he has a right [duty] to decline military service on the ground that he is entitled to insure that he honors his natural duty." One has, of course, not merely a right to honor his natural duty, but an obligation, a duty, to do so. And here, finally, Rawls follows his own logic and switches to the language of duty: "Actually, if the aims of the conflict are sufficiently dubious and the likelihood of receiving flagrantly unjust commands sufficiently great, one may have a duty and not only a right to refuse. Indeed, the conduct and aims of states in waging war, especially large and powerful ones, are in some circumstances so likely to be unjust that one is forced to conclude that in the foreseeable future one must abjure military service altogether." Rawls contrasts this with religious pacifism or religiously conscientious resistance to all wars, an otherworldly sectarian view that "no more challenges the state's authority than the celibacy of priests challenges the sanctity of marriage." [23]

Rawls does not ask what the fair penalty for doing one's natural duty and opposing predatory injustice should be. Surely it should not be very severe. In fact, we might conclude (or perhaps ought to conclude) that some incentive to do one's duty to help establish justice would be fair. Brian Barry criticizes Rawls for not paying enough attention to incentives and interests and the need to arrange structures of justice so that people will be motivated by their interests to do what is their natural duty, or what contributes to justice.[24] Barry's argument would apply to war as well: in a grievously unjust war fought for no good reason, in support of a dictator, opposed by the people, threatening to kill a million people if it continues, we would want incentives for massive numbers of people to resist the war for all sorts of motives so the war will end quickly.

Rawls does make some general suggestions about penalties. To decide on penalties, we would need to lift the veil of ignorance partially and move to a second stage, which can be called a constitutional convention stage. We would need to know the relevant facts about our society, its resources, economy, political culture, but would still have no information about particular individuals (including ourselves) and their relative status, abilities, and conception of the good. In other words, we could decide basic principles for our society without rigging it for ourselves or those who side with us. We would not know whether we would be the penalized or the penalizers.

What would be rational for us to decide concerning penalties? Rawls argues that we would establish penalties for one reason— for the sake of liberty. On the one hand we would want penalties to remove the grounds for thinking others are not complying with the rules and are causing a loss of liberty due to instability. On the other hand, we would want the loss of liberty due to penalties to be less than the loss of liberty from the instability they prevent.[25]

In an unjust war, a war not defending liberty but causing its loss, how much loss of liberty is caused by those who resist the war? Very little. In fact, if they can curtail the war, thereby curtailing the loss of liberty that the war is imposing, they cause a gain rather than a loss of liberty. The penalty, then, should be less than nothing.

The argument follows from the nature of the war and not from the ideology of the resister. Unlike the argument for toleration of conscientious refusal based on liberty of conscience, which depends on the conscientious motives of the resister, our argument is based on the desirability of any reasonable, nonviolent action, regardless of motive, which resists an unjust war. Clearly many who resisted the war, like many who prosecuted it, acted from mixed motives. Some were conscientious objectors, some objected selectively against this particular war, and many were also motivated by family needs, personal needs, and the pain and stress of warfare. Some, like Walter Davis, have gone farther in their dissent than a too-comfortable, over-forty professor such as the present writer. But the point is that fair punishment for the *act* of resistance against a war of this sort should be less than the penalty they have already paid. The argument applies to all nonviolent actions that resisted the war, including desertion, draft resistance, peace demonstrations, and noncriminal resistance actions that led to dishonorable discharges.

There is a third stage in Rawls's procedure—the legislative or policy stage. Here we still decide as if we were ignorant of our own position, but now we can add knowledge of political, economic, and social theories. This may help us consider when the decision can be made that a war is sufficiently unjust and oppressive that granting amnesty to resisters would be not only a healing of wounds but also fair to the resisters and fair to principles of liberty and justice.

After the nation has committed political, psychological, economic, and human resources to a war, it is difficult for the leaders who made the war policies to conclude publicly that they were wrong. That helps explain why amnesty has been granted more readily by a subsequent president rather than the war president. It is even difficult for a majority of the people, who have, after all, paid the price for the war, to conclude the war was unjust. They have invested too many emotions and lives, suffered too many wounds in the war, and there has been too much war propaganda and war spirit. Therefore when a war is in fact unjust, the indications are usually indirect: the war's divisiveness, the polls showing that many feel entry into the war was a mistake, or perhaps the defeat of the incumbent president's party in an election in which the war was a decisive issue.

We have noted before that presidents have usually granted amnesty not in the name of fairness, but in the name of peace and the public good and the need to bind up the wounds and heal the divisions and the strife. We have agreed that, in the tragedy of war, those reasons supersede the question of fairness. Now we are noticing that the divisions and strife indicate there may have been good reason for some to resist the war. Thus divisions and strife are practical indicators that amnesty will not only serve a healing function, but will also be fair to the natural duty of justice. Traditional wisdom and our novel argument tend to converge in practice.

This may help explain why presidents have granted amnesty more readily in our history when the war was particularly divisive, or when a significant segment of the people opposed the government's policies. George Washington, for example, was quick and generous in granting amnesty after the Whiskey Rebellion. So were Abraham Lincoln and Andrew Johnson during and after the Civil War, Lincoln not even waiting until the war was over to begin declaring partial amnesties. These presidents did not require that the majority should conclude the war was wrong or even that they themselves should believe the war was wrong, but moved to heal the divisiveness arising because a significant portion of the population believed it was wrong. And this may help explain why since World War II there has been a departure from the tradition of amnesty established by presidents from Washington through Roosevelt. In World War II, the proportion of the people who felt the war was a mistake stayed under 15 percent. In the wake of that war the image of draft resistance changed, and there was a departure from the usual tradition of amnesty. The departure carried through the Korean war and is partly still with us. By contrast, 76 percent of the population now feel the Vietnam war was a mistake, and less than 20 percent feel it was not a mistake.[26] We may be nearing the time when we will return to the practices that prevailed before World War II. In sum, history suggests that there has been some rough correlation between the reduction of penalties for resistance and the feeling by a significant segment of the population that the war was a mistake. Our "novel conclusion" may be not so novel as it might sound.

What penalty is heavy enough in an unjust war? What penalty has been paid by resisters during the Vietnam war? Career disruption was one part of the penalty. Students well on their way to a successful career lost contacts in their home area, and with the liability of being somewhat foreign and somewhat suspect, were often unemployed for a long time until finally finding semi-skilled jobs. There was considerable loss of momentum and opportunity. There was also the loss of contact with friends, relatives, hometown, nation. Exiles may not come home even for a parent's funeral without likelihood of arrest. The initial anguish over making a decision many of us had been taught to scorn was a penalty, as was the initial risk that one's fellow citizens and friends might not eventually conclude that the war was a mistake, and might reject one's decision and oneself. Finally there was the loss of the political liberties to participate in the nation's political process.

Penalties of a similar nature are paid by deserters as well as draft resisters, of course. And those who did not desert, but resisted while in the armed service and received less than honorable discharges, pay other penalties.

Surely these penalties are heavy enough in an unjust war. We concluded earlier that fairness dictates some incentive to encourage resistance against an unjust war. Clearly that would suggest penalties of a shorter duration than resisters have had to pay in the Vietnam war. We concluded that the natural duty of justice required people to resist an unjust war, and that justice is served by encouraging them to do so. The penalty of banishment cuts off their ability to do so. Their act of leaving by the tens of thousands was a dramatic witness against the war, but their continuing banishment violates the main thrust of the logic we have followed. In an unjust war, the voices of resisters are badly needed. Yet the draft system coerced them to muffle their dissent prior to induction because draft boards might single them out for induction; it coerced them to limit their free speech to small, trusted groups after receiving the draft call lest the authorities learn of their plans to refuse; and it erected powerful barriers of long jail terms or banishment, removing them from any audiences in this country which could have heard their speech. That penalty is the opposite of what is needed in an unjust war.

What about the case of the just war? What penalty is appropriate there? We concluded that the penalty should not be so small as to encourage many to shirk their share of the duty. In a war like World War II, the penalties automatically become more severe without additional government action. Those who resisted were resisting a just war against the Nazis, and the loss of friends, families, and careers is much more bitter and hostile; the anxiety of the decision and the risk of never returning home become much greater. Furthermore, in a just war, there is great psychological pressure against shirkers, and a great rallying to support the effort. Many who are not drafted volunteer, and few refuse the draft. These penalties have been sufficient to support the war effort in our history, even in some wars we should not have fought, in spite of the precedent of twenty-eight amnesties of various sorts. Therefore we may conclude that the precedent of granting amnesties after most wars has not been excessively lenient.

Hannah Arendt writes of the banality of evil in Eichmann, who could obediently commit evil on a gigantic scale without thinking, without conscience, without the thought occurring to him that perhaps he should question, dissent, and disobey. He relied on "clichés, stock phrases, adherence to conventional, standardized codes of expression and conduct," and this allowed him to ignore the claims of reality, conscience, and the duty of justice. Arendt then writes of the value of thinking and dissent:

> When everybody is swept away unthinkingly by what everybody else does and believes in, those who think are drawn out of hiding because their refusal to join is conspicuous and thereby becomes a kind of action. The purging element in thinking, Socrates' midwifery, that brings out the implications of unexamined opinions and thereby destroys them—values, doctrines, theories, and even convictions—is political by implication. For this destruction has a liberating effect on another human faculty, the faculty of judgment, which one may call, with some justification, the most political of man's mental abilities.[27]

If Arendt is right, and if thinking has some part in education, then educational institutions have good reason to support the right and the duty to dissent. Not only education, but democracy does. For however just the constitution, there is always the likelihood that those who govern will depart from justice and travel into banality. Then conscientious refusal becomes not a threat to justice and stable democracy but an instrument of its restoration.[28]

That is why, behind the veil of ignorance, we would qualify the obligation to obey the law with the natural duty of justice. We would not remove from ourselves the possibility that in a situation of sufficient injustice, "a citizen is justified in refusing to discharge his legal duty." In an unjust war, "he has a right to decline military service on the ground that he is entitled to insure that he honors his natural duty." And in cases of this sort, authorities should "reduce and in some cases suspend the legal sanction" or penalty.[29] Fortunately, the United States constitution grants the power of pardon explicitly to the president and implicitly to the Congress, and the historical precedent in the

United States is that twenty-eight amnesties of various sorts have been granted after wars.

The argument that it is the natural duty of justice to resist an unjust war sheds light on the concern of some like James Finn that resisters should do something to express their political obligation as citizens.[30] With the aid of John Rawls, we have seen that resistance against an unjust war is not only a liberty enjoyed by an individual conscience, as Finn speaks of it. The principles of a just war on the basis of which the resistance occurs are principles at the basis of any just state. They are the teachings of a long tradition, and they are also the principles that a fair decision process would conclude to be the natural duty, the political obligation, of any person. Resisters consciously undertake to perform an act which risks the penalties that resisters pay. They perform the act out of a sense of political obligation. It is no accident that so many resisters had already demonstrated more than the average sense of political obligation. That act of resistance, justified by the natural duty of justice, and paid for at considerable cost, was in fact a strong demonstration of political obligation. Its cost was less than that paid by those who lost limbs and lives in Vietnam, but more than most of us paid.

And that turns the argument toward the rest of us who are concerned about power and empowerment in education. The duty that falls on the draftee to resist injustice is a natural duty that belongs to everyone. The resisters, like everyone else, acted out of a mixture of motives. One motive was their sense of duty to establish a process of education for the nation. Do we have a parallel duty to establish fairness for resisters, so that they are not permanently banished from the process of dissent? It was a law professor at the University of Tennessee who finally proved that the rejection of Walter Davis's application for status as a conscientious objector was illegal, and thereby won him the right to return home. As the resisters' initial decisions were part of a community of discussion, so their restoration will only come as part of a shared effort from the communities whose progeny they are. It is a natural duty, and in fairness it should be shared equally by the rest of us in the community, without shirking. Michael Walzer put it rightly in his essay, "The Obligation to Disobey."

The heroic encounter between sovereign individual and sovereign state, if it ever took place, would be terrifyingly unequal. . . . it is not the mere individual right to rebel . . . that sustains the enterprise but, rather, the mutual undertakings of the participants. Without this mutuality, very few men would ever join the "contest"—not because of the fear of being killed but because of the greater fear of being alone. "This is what is most difficult," wrote Jean Le Meur, the young French army officer who was imprisoned for refusing to fight in Algeria, "being cut off from the fraternity, being locked up in a monologue, being incomprehensible." And then: "Do tell the others that this is not a time to let me down." [31]

NOTES

1. Murray Polner, *When Can I Come Home?* (New York: Doubleday, 1972), p. 95.

2. Douglas W. Jones and David L. Raish, "American Deserters and Draft Evaders: Exile, Punishment or Amnesty?" *Harvard International Law Journal* 13 (Winter 1972): 88–89; Robert K. Musil, "The Truth about Deserters," *The Nation*, 16 April 1973, CCCO reprint, pp. 2 and 5–6; *Amex-Canada*, October-November 1975, p. 4; "Amnesty Fact Sheet," Mimeographed (Washington, D.C.: National Interreligious Service Board for Conscientious Objectors, Jan. 19, 1976).

3. John P. Martha, "Draft Resisters and Deserters," *American Legion*, July 1974, p. 18.

4. Julian C. Carey, "Amnesty: An Act of Grace," *Saint Louis University Law Journal* 17 (1972–1973): 517–18.

5. Polner, *When Can I Come Home?*, p. 143 (italics mine).

6. Ibid., p. 65.

7. William D. Wick, "The Case for an Unconditional, Universal Amnesty for Draft Evaders and Armed Forces Deserters," *Buffalo Law Review*, Fall 1972, pp. 333–34; John Swomley, Jr., "Amnesty and Reconciliation," *Christian Century*, 27 December 1972, pp. 1322–24; James F. Childress, "The Amnesty Argument," *Cross Currents*, Fall 1973, p. 322. I am indebted to James Childress, David Little, and Kathy Heatherly for their helpful comments at several points in the evolution of my argument.

8. Charles Lutz, "Amnesty as Value Clarification for Christians," *Christian Century*, 2 October 1974, p. 905.

9. John Rawls, *A Theory of Justice* (Cambridge, Mass.: Harvard University Press, 1971).

10. Ibid., p. 11.

11. Ibid., p. 12.

12. William A. Rusher, "Amnesty? Never!" in Arlie Schardt, William Rusher, and Mark Hatfield, *Amnesty? The Unsettled Question of Vietnam* (Croton-on-Hudson, N.Y.: Sun River Press, 1973), pp. 58–59, 88.

13. Rawls, *Theory of Justice*, p. 334.

14. Ibid., pp. 336, 337.

15. Polner, *When Can I Come Home?*, pp. 62, 126, 209–10.

16. Rawls, *Theory of Justice*, pp. 206–7 (cf. pp. 220–21), 206n, 60.

17. Ibid., pp. 214–15.

18. Ibid., pp. 368–69.

19. Ibid., pp. 380–81.

20. Ibid., p. 370.

21. Richmond, Va., John Knox Press, 1969.

22. Rawls, *Theory of Justice*, p. 380.

23. Ibid., p. 381.

24. Brian Barry, *The Liberal Theory of Justice: A Critical Examination of the Principal Doctrines in* A Theory of Justice *by John Rawls* (London: Oxford, Clarendon Press, 1973).

25. Rawls, *Theory of Justice*, pp. 240–41; cf. p. 215.

26. Harris Poll, March 20, 1975.

27. Hannah Arendt, "Thinking and Moral Considerations," *Social Research*, Autumn 1971, pp. 417–18 and 445–46.

28. Rawls, *Theory of Justice*, pp. 383, 381, 387.

29. Ibid., pp. 381, 387.

30. James Finn, "The Amnesty Issue," *Commonweal*, 3 November 1972, pp. 105–8.

31. Michael Walzer, "The Obligation to Disobey," in his *Obligations: Essays on Disobedience, War, and Citizenship* (Cambridge, Mass.: Harvard University Press, 1970), p. 22.

Comparative Politics of Education in Four Industrial Nations

NACK YOUNG AN

Antistatist attitudes have held sway in the United States for many years, and as a consequence active governmental involvement in the provision of social services has often been looked at askance. The machinery of government in the United States has not been considered an instrument to be used casually but only in the most extreme circumstances. Excessive government is believed to endanger liberty; in addition, private enterprise is believed to be more efficient than government, and government is expected to encourage private initiative and free competition. The United States consequently has lagged considerably behind other industrial nations in the area of welfare services. Education, however, is an exception to this general state of affairs. Governmental power has been employed deliberately and consistently to strengthen higher education. The government has been one of the major enabling powers for education—through policy, law, and heavy funding.

The major tasks addressed in this paper are: the illustration of the foregoing proposition with reference to the varying levels of governmental activities, including the provision for education in the United States, the United Kingdom, West Germany, and France; a survey of the literature attempting to explore variables that account for the different levels of legislative innovation in different political units; and the presentation of our own explanation of why public support for education varies so much in the four countries.

In all the important service areas, such as old-age pensions, unemployment insurance, sick pay, and medical services, the

United States was the last of the four countries under study to introduce government activity. While Germany introduced old-age pensions and unemployment insurance in 1889 and 1927 respectively, the United States did not introduce either until 1935. Great Britain began public medical services as early as 1911, but only in 1965 did the United States introduce a government insurance scheme ("Medicare") providing hospital insurance for those aged sixty-five or over.[1]

Not only the date of introduction of various services, but also the level of expenditure, measured in terms of social security expenditure as a percentage of gross national product, clearly supports the premise that the United States government has opposed social welfare expenditure except for education. American public expenditures for civilian health programs, for instance, did not grow noticeably in relation to GNP for a half century. The National Board of Health was still a mere fledgling in 1883, and until 1953 the Public Health Service was administered by the Treasury Department.[2]

American public housing too has been a stagnant and token program. Public housing and low-income housing subsidies constituted .05 percent of gross national product in 1936 and the same in 1965. Public child-welfare services have expanded and contracted in erratic patterns, rather than registering a consistent growth rate.[3]

Public health expenditures in the United States constituted .45 percent of gross national product in 1913, and in 1932 they still accounted for only .7 percent of gross national product. Between 1950 and the early 1960s, the share of social security expenditures accounted for by public health service programs declined from about 10 percent to 5.6 percent in the United States.[4]

A similar pattern is discernible also in old-age pensions and unemployment insurance, in that the United States appears to be the only country in which, although a majority of the aged receive state pensions, a substantial minority do not. As the result of successive extensions of the 1935 social security scheme, about 90 percent of the population is now eligible to receive a government pension on retirement, but the proportion of those over sixty-five receiving such pensions as late as 1971 was considerably lower—perhaps on the order of 60–70 percent.[5]

The same appears true with unemployment insurance. In the United States the benefits represent fairly consistently the lowest percentage of regular earnings, and the periods during which the benefit is payable are the shortest, of any of the four countries compared. The average benefit in the United States seems to be about 30 percent of regular earnings, payable for about twenty-six weeks.[6]

An entirely opposite pattern emerges with regard to education, however. American commitment to education as a desirable public good is so firmly established that it has the semblance of a religion, and the general diffusion of literacy has been considered a virtue from the earliest days of the Republic. Religious leaders in the early days emphasized education as a necessary vehicle for disseminating religious dogmas. The affirmation of the individual's personal relation to God and the importance of reading the Bible caused Calvinists to emphasize elementary education for all children. As early as 1647 the General Court of Massachusetts required all towns of a certain size to establish and maintain reading schools. By the time of the American Revolution it is estimated that 90 to 95 percent of the white inhabitants of the New England colonies were at least literate, a level which was not achieved by any area in Europe, with the exception of Scotland, until the late nineteenth century.[7]

As the nation undertook the task of self-government, whose success depends upon an enlightened electorate, the fervor for education grew more intense. The land ordinance of 1785 reserved one lot in each township for public schools, and the Northwest Ordinance decreed that "religion, morality, and knowledge being necessary to good government . . . , schools and the means of education shall forever be encouraged." George Washington's *Farewell Address* admonished the people to promote "as an object of primary importance, institutions for the general diffusion of knowledge." [8] Jefferson, too, believed that the successful operation of democracy depended to a significant extent upon the education of the populace. He espoused a broad system of public education as a means to reduce the effects of demagoguery; in proposing a bill for an extensive system of public education in Virginia, he noted that not only would such a system train useful leaders, but the people generally would also be better able to discern tyranny in its different forms. Ignorance was thus considered an impediment to the effective operation of a popular democracy. Education in the principles of republicanism was essential in his scheme; but it was also "the resource most to be relied on for ameliorating the condition, promoting the virtue, and advancing the happiness of man." [9]

The founding of the University of Virginia indicates the importance Jefferson attached to public secular education in a free society. He attached so much importance to higher education that he perceived benefits accruing from centralization in university education and from the concentration of state aid upon higher educational interests. For Jefferson the state had a stake in the education of its people because education is the business of the state which is essential to the happiness, prosperity, and liberty of the people, and it is for the maintenance and promotion of these that the state exists.

This is by no means to suggest that the democratic educational ideal either became a commonplace of American social thought or was put into common practice during Jefferson's time. On the contrary, it was many decades before the ideal took on real meaning.

Only after the Civil War did the United States approach the creation of a general system of compulsory primary education. Even then only a tiny percentage of the nation's children so much as began secondary school. The working class usually treated secondary school as an upper-class institution, one irrelevant to their own aspirations and difficult for them to use because of the importance of adolescent earnings. Only in the early 1900s did American secondary education begin a rapid expansion, as evinced by the fact that the percentage of American 14-to-17-year-olds attending secondary schools full time nearly quintupled from 6.7 percent in 1890 to 32.3 in 1920. By the 1920s the secondary school had come to be looked upon as an integral part of the school system for children—with little regard to their social, economic, or intellectual status. By 1928 the proportion of this

Secondary School Enrollment per 10,000 Population

Year	United States	West Germany	United Kingdom	France
1920	247	117	83	38
1930	388	110	115	45
1946	581	205	283	181
1960	571	231	673	363
1966	588	226	651	850

age group attending general or academic secondary schools full time was five times higher in the United States than in Europe.[10]

In terms of age-cohort proportions enrolled in secondary schools, the United States passed the 10 percent mark about 1910, Europe generally not until after 1945; the 30 percent mark was passed by the United States in the early 1920s, in Europe not until the 1960s. The enrollment in all secondary schools per 10,000 of population was higher in the United States until the immediate post–World War II era than in European countries, as shown in the accompanying table.[11]

The contrast is even more pronounced in higher education: the proportion of the appropriate groups attending institutions of higher learning in the United States is far larger than in the European countries.

In the United States, the evolution of the university was rather different from that of the primary and secondary schools. Until the 1860s, universities adhered closely to the upper-class values of British institutions and were attended only by a small elite. But with the establishment of the land-grant colleges, which introduced scientific and technical training, universities became extremely popular.

In the 1950s for every 100,000 of population, 1,738 were enrolled in colleges and universities in the United States, 1,101 in West Germany, 256 in the United Kingdom, and 409 in France. In 1966, 43 percent of the United States population between twenty and twenty-four years of age were students, as contrasted with 7.5 percent in West Germany, 7 percent in the United Kingdom, and 16 percent in France.[12]

The relative per-pupil expenditures on education in the four

countries are in keeping with the general pattern that the United
States does more for education than other countries do, spending
over twice as much on each elementary pupil in 1970 as West
Germany, her nearest competitor, and outspending the other
three nations by smaller margins on the university level.[13]

The preeminence of the United States in the educational
spending pattern is obvious also in terms of the expenditures in
relationship to the GNP. In 1969, for example, expenditures for
education were 6.3 percent of the GNP in the United States, 3.6
percent in West Germany, 5.6 percent in the United Kingdom,
and 4.5 percent in France.[14]

Federal efforts in the field of higher education in the United
States throughout the years are equally noteworthy. Federal land
grants were made from time to time for the support of higher
education (a federal land grant helped establish Miami University of Ohio in 1809, for example), and finally the famous Morrill
Act was passed in 1862. This historic measure set aside areas in
the several states for the creation and support of the great land-
grant colleges that have played so important an educational role
in the nation. This was followed in 1865 by further grants to
finance agricultural experiment stations, which have received
continuing federal subsidies ever since.

After World War II the federal government appropriated over
$14 billion to help millions of veterans finance a college education.
Moreover, after the Sputniks prompted reports that the Soviet
Union was producing far more engineers than the United
States—as many technically trained personnel as Western Europe
and the United States combined—Congress passed the National
Defense Education Act in 1958. Under this act, hundreds of
millions of dollars have been spent for a variety of purposes
believed to be related to national defense. Money has been contributed in the form of grants to universities establishing or expanding graduate programs, scholarships for students doing
graduate work in certain fields, aid to students planning to enter
the teaching profession, loans to college students unable to finance
their own education, and assistance in financing laboratory
equipment and remodeling classrooms for the teaching of
mathematics, science, and modern foreign languages.

In addition, a number of major universities now receive over half their income from federal grants. The federal government has advanced hundreds of millions of dollars in low-interest loans to colleges for dormitory construction since 1950. It supports Howard University as well as Federal City College in Washington.

In contrast, the provision of education as a public good by government in Europe is a relatively new development. Education was initially provided by the Roman Catholic Church and was used primarily as a vehicle for the propagation of Christian doctrine. Education was directed to preparing young men for the priesthood; it was primarily moral and disciplinary rather than intellectual. Formal education was reserved for the few. Indeed, until the mid-twentieth century, education in most European countries remained segregated by social class. Most people received an elementary education and then some vocational training until they were fifteen or sixteen years old. Relatively few went from special elementary schools to public or grammar schools in England, to Gymnasia in Germany, or Lycées in France; and a still smaller number went on to the university or its equivalent.[15]

However, as societies become more highly differentiated and complex, socializing agencies other than the family become more important. Skills must be taught which require specialized instruction. Formal schooling becomes imperative for those destined to become the guardians of the society's heritage and members of its bureaucracy. Moreover, if a society is to mobilize its resources to the fullest and create an industrial culture, education must be extended to many. Not only is widespread literacy essential, but the number of required specialized skills that cannot be taught in the home or through apprenticeship increases geometrically. Technological growth has reached the point that only those who are professionally dedicated to mastering fairly limited aspects of the new sciences can provide the requisite training for a new generation. And as competence in technical fields is essential to the industrial society, education has come to be accepted as a prime source of mobilization of the society. The connection between literacy and national power has become more and more obvious as technology has advanced, and nation-states have moved to centralize the control of education in their hands. This general pattern has been noticeable in all the industrialized societies, but most visibly so in the countries under study; it would be useful to sketch the development patterns in those countries.

Until 1833 the English state had hardly anything to do with the educational process. What education the poor received was provided by church schools, the charity of philanthropists, or apprenticeship. The rich were educated by tutors or at exclusive private or church schools. In 1833, however, Parliament authorized the use of money "in aid of private subscriptions for the education of the poor classes," and in 1880 it made elementary education compulsory. Consequently, 1,500,000 children out of 1,700,000 were attending school in 1935 and by 1961, the figure was 2,500,000 out of 2,750,000. These figures compare very favorably with 875,000 children out of a possible 1,500,000 for the year 1816. The amount of schooling also increased: the average duration of school attendance in 1835 was one year and by 1851 it had risen to two years. In 1893, the terminal age for education was fixed at eleven; in 1918 this was raised to fourteen. The pattern of improvement persisted, but the next major piece of educational legislation was not adopted until 1944.[16]

In that year Parliament divided the national educational institutions into elementary and secondary schools and created scholarships to enable students to enter some of the better private schools and universities. The new law established three categories of secondary schools: grammar schools, to provide primarily academic training for university attendance; modern schools, to offer both general and vocational training; and technical schools, to equip students with the skills needed in industry. As late as 1963 close to 60 percent of the school children between twelve and fifteen were attending modern schools, many of them leaving school at fifteen. But opportunities have broadened in the United Kingdom since World War II. More and more young people are entering college-preparatory programs as the movement toward the comprehensive school so characteristic of the United States gains ground. Even education at Oxford and Cambridge, which used to be a confirmation of status and the only channel of social mobility, is accessible to sons and daughters of manual workers.

While there were fewer students attending universities in the United Kingdom than on the Continent, the proportion enrolled from the lower classes was greater there than on the Continent. England has always been a less stratified society than either Germany or France; in the 1940s, for example, 23 percent of British university students were sons and daughters of manual workers, as compared with about 4 percent in Germany and France.[17]

Despite some attempts by the French government to expand educational facilities in the seventeenth and eighteenth centuries, most schools had been maintained by the Church and catered primarily to the well-to-do or those in religious orders. Nor did there develop in France that tradition of philanthropy or concern with the education of the indigent that was an English hallmark.

Consequently, at the time of the French Revolution, three-fourths of the women and more than half of the men in France were illiterate.[18] However, the system of public primary schools slowly grew, and in the later nineteenth century, the goal of primary education for all was implemented under the Third Republic. In 1881 compulsory schooling for children between the ages of six and thirteen became law. The democratization and expansion of higher education in the postwar years was evident in the increase of the proportion of eligible students receiving diplomas from secondary schools. It jumped from 5 percent in 1950 to 11.5 percent in 1960 and was expected to reach 23.5 percent in 1970. The de Gaulle government carried its commitment further by raising the terminal school age from fourteen to sixteen.[19]

Despite the fact that Prussia was the first major European power to enunciate the idea of universal elementary education, the state did not immediately commit massive resources to the education of German youth. As late as 1911, more than 90 percent of the students attended an elementary school (*Volksschule*) until age fourteen, after which they found employment or entered an apprenticeship. Some states of the empire provided for a minimum of 240 hours of continuation school for those from fourteen through seventeen. A few students, drawn almost entirely from the middle classes and the aristocracy, entered a three-year preparatory school at age six and then continued their education for nine years at a Gymnasium. Graduation from a Gymnasium and passage of an entrance examination were required for admission to a university.[20]

This educational system has divided Germans into two distinct groups: the educated (*Gebildete*) and those who have had no chance for more than a grade-school education. Education has been the property of an elite, small compared to the masses of the *Ungebildete*. Membership in this elite was attained not on the basis of selection of talent through equal opportunity but through the educational monopoly enjoyed by the financially able.[21]

The evidence presented thus far clearly indicates that education has been extolled as a desirable public good in the United States more than in the European countries. The question of what accounts for variance in endeavors by different political systems in a given policy area is an intriguing one. Political scientists have devoted much scholarly effort to the task of identifying variables that closely correlate with policy outputs. Especially notable research in this area has been done by students of American politics.

Among variables that are frequently identified as the sources of policy output, the so-called socioeconomic and the political variables are outstanding—the former encompassing such variables as urbanization, industrialization, income, and education, the latter including voter registration, legislative malapportionment, party control of state government, party competition, governor's powers, legislative professionalism, legal professionalism, administrative professionalism, and voter turnout.

Various researchers, without reaching a consensus, have singled out one or more of those variables as significant factors in influencing policy innovation. Thomas Dye suggests that characteristics of the political system have relatively little independent effect on policy outcomes in the states, contending that economic development shapes both political systems and political outcomes.[22]

In a similar vein, Herbert Jacob found no visible effect of malapportionment on policy outcomes. He observes that if malapportionment has a widespread effect on state politics, it is a good deal more subtle than we have hitherto assumed. Dye's work on a similar topic produced a conclusion supporting Jacob's finding. Dye notes that policies which might be heavily favored by the often underrepresented urban majority were not more evident in well-apportioned states than in poorly apportioned states, the substantial differences in the level of outputs being accounted for by a variety of other variables.[23]

By the same token, Dawson and Robinson found the degree of party competition to be an insignificant factor. Competitive states were not more liberal in welfare and education expenditures when the socioeconomic variables were held constant. Hofferbert, summing up the preceding studies, concludes that party competition, divided party control between governors and their legislatures, and apportionment have little influence on policy output.[24]

On the other hand, the preceding position has been attacked by those who still believe that "politics" has an important impact on public policy, a position well supported by such classic case studies as those by V. O. Key, Duane Lockard, and Charles Adrian, to name but a few.[25]

Pointing out the limitations of the position that analysis of characteristics of a political system will not explain policy outputs, Jacob and Lipsky succinctly point out that such socioeconomic variables as income, urbanization, industrialization, and education have little substantive relationship to inputs.[26] They point out that one may conceive of these socioeconomic measures as environmental factors which may lead to the articulation of demands from and supports to the political system, but that demands and supports, as inputs, are behavioral articulations of satisfaction or dissatisfaction with the way things are.

Clarke, criticizing from a slightly different perspective, points out that the emphasis upon socioeconomic variables is a product of methodology or a result of attaching too much significance to the analysis of revenue and expenditure policies that are quite likely dependent on variables indicative of the economic potential or tax base of states. Fry and Winters, on the other hand, concern themselves with the general question of whether or not the political system exercises an important impact on public policy outcomes. They focus their analysis on the "redistribution of policy benefits or sanctions" and believe this to be a significant policy dimension for political science, since much of the conflict preceding adoption of a program is not about whether it should be embarked upon but about who will pay and who will benefit. They conclude their study by noting that in regard to the allocation of the burdens and benefits of state government revenues and expenditures, political variables will have a stronger influence than will socioeconomic variables.[27]

While no universally accepted variable that satisfactorily accounts for policy innovation in the several states exists, certain other variables have been carefully scrutinized in attempts to explain policy differences between the United States and the European countries, with particular reference to elites, demands, interest groups, and institutions.[28]

According to one proposition, government plays a smaller role in the United States because, unlike the other countries, the United States government is controlled by an elite that successfully inhibits the expansion of state activity. If this argument is to be held valid, it has to be proved that the United States is the only one of the four countries dominated by an elite, or that the American elite is alone in wishing to limit the sphere of the state and in succeeding in doing so. This line of argument is not very convincing, because America is not the only industrial country whose power structure has been interpreted in the manner of C. Wright Mills.[29] It will be difficult to accept the view that the American elite is more successful than the others in imposing its will, or in flouting the will of others.

According to another argument, governments in the United States have done little because the American public has not demanded expansions of state activity. Implicit in this is the idea that the masses in other countries have demanded and gotten expansions of state activity, or that in any or all of the other countries governments do things whether or not they are demanded, while in the United States governments act only on demand and are more amenable to public opinion than in other countries.

It is difficult to think of any act of nationalization in Europe as a result of extensive public demand for it. The British case is probably most illustrative. It is believed that the Labor Party won the 1945 general election only in spite of its commitments to nationalization, and that most voters remained rather indifferent to the Labor Government's subsequent nationalization measures.[30] However, popular majorities at most times in all of the four countries have demanded the extension of existing social services and the establishment of new ones. Sixty-two percent of the American public, for instance, favored federal aid to education and sixty-three percent a hospital insurance scheme for the aged.[31]

Another proposition holds that government plays a more limited role in the United States because American interest groups, unlike their European counterparts, have prevented government from assuming a greater role. Interest groups are seen to be in possession of more politically effective resources in the United States than in other countries. Actually, however, interest groups in other countries have similar resources at their disposal, such as leadership skills, knowledge, numbers, access to the media of communication, and the sanction of withdrawing their cooperation; in some cases, they are more effective than interest groups in the United States.

Those who view institutions as a variable try to relate the structure and functioning of American institutions to the level of government activity. They contend that the American political system has unusual institutional features that tend to maximize the probability that any given proposal for a policy change will be rejected or deferred. The difficulty with this contention is that those institutional obstacles such as federalism, separation of powers, the constitutional position of the Supreme Court, and the part played by congressional committees can be surmounted, as shown by the American experience that almost all of the major innovations in policy have been concentrated in a small number of congresses: Roosevelt's first three and the Eighty-ninth elected with Johnson in 1964. Moreover, what distinguished those congresses was not the absence of procedural obstacles but the presence of determined reformist majorities.

Some scholars have attempted to relate the level of government activity to such variables as the professionalization of bureaucracy, the length of experiment with social welfare programs, and geographical contiguity. A convincing argument has been made with respect to the significance of the dates of the introduction of civil service reform. The British Northcote-Trevelyan reform movement in the 1850s preceded the initiation of American federal reforms through the Pendleton Act (1883) by a generation. During the Progressive era, mistrust of the probity and efficiency of public officialdom was frequently used by those who were opposed to public sector expansion on ideological and public-interest grounds. The reforms of the Progressive period were not associated with confidence in existing governmental agencies as capable of administering social programs.

Correlation between the level of government activity and the length of experience with welfare programs has also been explored: the longer the country has had them, the higher is the level of government activity in welfare programs.[32] In a similar vein, geographical contiguity has also proven to be a significant variable: the closer a country is to other countries with highly developed welfare systems, the higher is the level of government activity in welfare programs.[33]

However plausible and convincing, none of the theories we have examined so far explains the extraordinary efforts the United States has made in the field of education. What makes the case of education clearly the chief exception to the American policy pattern? Education has been a means to reconcile the dilemma posed by the two equally important American cultural values—equality, with the provision of opportunities for upward social mobility, and a highly individualistic social order. This gigantic task could be undertaken by the state on economic grounds without competing, except in a very small way, with the private sector.

What really buttressed the state's position, however, was the desire of native-born Americans to "Americanize" succeeding waves of immigrants. By 1900 immigration had brought to America a large number of non-English-speaking, unskilled eastern and southern Europeans. Many educators hoped that whether or not the immigrants could excel in traditional subjects, they could equal their classmates in their adherence to a democratic social life beyond the classroom. Moreover, if the immigrants could prove themselves to be "good Americans," they might find less resistance to their nascent demands for acceptance into the American mainstream. In other words, a major objective of the educators' quest was to transform the immigrant working class into American-style democrats.

Public education, therefore, consistently aimed at achieving Anglo-Saxon conformity. Generally, immigrants were viewed with suspicious ambivalence, wanted for their muscle power but unwanted because of their foreignness. As long ago as 1794 George Washington, writing to John Adams, questioned the value of free immigration, because immigrants retain the language, habits, and principles (good or bad) which they bring with them. Jefferson also feared mass immigration, for fear that "the importation of foreigners" would lead to a sharing of political power, wherein they would infuse legislation with a foreign "spirit, warp and bias its directions, and render it a heterogeneous, incoherent, and distracted mass." [34] The educational goal projected for immigrant students, therefore, was to remold them in the image of the founding fathers.

The task of education, wrote an educator as late as 1909, is to "break up these [immigrant] groups or settlements, to assimilate and amalgamate these people as part of our American race, and to implant in their children, so far as can be done, the Anglo-Saxon conception of righteousness, law and order, and popular government, and to awaken in them a reverence for our democratic institutions and for those things in our national life which we as a people hold to be of abiding worth." [35] To meet this objective a number of schools began to offer civics courses, the purpose of which was to develop in all students an allegiance to democratic citizenship. Indeed the socialization of the stream of non–North European immigrants and their inculcation with values and skills approved by future employers have been among the important tasks of the state. These were not tasks that could safely be left to private institutions, since private institutions in practice would have meant (and sometimes did mean) the immigrant communities themselves. Consequently, "as keeper and official inculcator of the amalgam of economic and idealistic values later identified as the American Way of Life, the public school was the closest approximation to an American established church." [36]

It would be difficult to explain the massive governmental efforts in the area of education in the United States with any one of the socioeconomic or other variables mentioned. A more acceptable explanation may be found in that peculiarly American ideology that emphasizes the importance of an enlightened electorate as a prerequisite to democratic government, and in the extraordinary exigencies that necessitated massive public efforts to inculcate American values and norms among the waves of immigrants.

NOTES

1. See the chart in Anthony King, "Ideas, Institutions and the Policies of Governments," *Science* 3, pt. 3 (July 1973): 300.
2. Statistical Office of the European Communities, *Basic Statistics of the Community*, 1971, p. 104; Ida C. Merriam and Alfred M. Skolnik, *Social Welfare Expenditures under Public Programs in the United States, 1929–1966* (Washington, D.C.: United States Social Security Administration, 1968), p. 253.
3. Merriam and Skolnik, *Social Welfare Expenditures*, pp. 161, 253.
4. *The Cost of Social Security: Sixth International Inquiry* (Geneva: International Labor Office, 1967), p. 322.
5. King, "Ideas," p. 297.
6. Ibid., p. 298.
7. Stanley Rothman, *European Society and Politics* (Indianapolis, Ind.: Bobbs-Merrill, 1970), p. 236.
8. Rush Welter, *Popular Education and Democratic Thought in America* (New York: Columbia University Press, 1962), p. 25.
9. Alan Pendleton Crimes, *American Political Thought* (New York: Holt, Rinehart and Winston, 1960), p. 152; quotation in A. J. Beitzinger, *A History of American Political Thought* (New York: Dodd, Mead, 1972), p. 277.
10. Isaac Leon Kandel, ed., *Twenty-Five Years of American Education* (New York: Macmillan, 1924), p. 267; N. Hans, "Comparative Educational Statistics," in *Yearbook of Education: 1934* (London: Evans, 1935), pp. 172–73, 180–83.
11. Arthur S. Banks, ed., *Cross-Polity Times-Series Data* (Cambridge: M.I.T. Press, 1971), segment 6.
12. UNESCO, *World Survey of Education*, vol. 4 (Paris:

UNESCO, 1964); Dimitri Chorafas, *The Knowledge Revolution* (London: George Allen and Unwin, 1969).

13. UNESCO, *Statistical Yearbook, 1967* (Paris, 1968), p. 556.

14. Ibid.

15. Dimitri Chorafas, *Knowledge Revolution*.

16. Raymond Williams, *The Long Revolution* (New York: Columbia University Press, 1961), pp. 136–37.

17. Joseph Ben-David, "Professions in the Class System of Present Day Societies," *Current Sociology* 12, no. 3 (1963–1964): 285–86.

18. Rothman, *European Society and Politics*, p. 243.

19. George A. Male, *Education in France* (Washington, D.C.: U.S. Department of Health, Education and Welfare, 1963), p. 163.

20. Rothman, *European Society and Politics*, pp. 248–51.

21. John H. Herz, *The Government of Germany* (New York: Harcourt Brace Jovanovich, 1972), pp. 14–17.

22. Thomas Dye, *Politics, Economics, and the Public Policy in American States* (Chicago: Rand McNally, 1966), pp. 4–5.

23. Herbert Jacob, "The Consequences of Malapportionment: A Note of Caution," *Social Forces* 48 (1964): 256–61; Thomas Dye, "Malapportionment and Public Policy in the States," *Journal of Politics* 27 (1965): 586–602.

24. Richard E. Dawson and James A. Robinson, "Inter-party Competition, Economic Variables and Welfare Policies in the American States," *Journal of Politics* 25 (1963): 265–89; Richard Hofferbert, "The Relation between Public Policy and Some Structural and Environmental Variables in the American States," *American Political Science Review* 9 (1966): 73–82.

25. V. O. Key, *American State Politics* (New York: Alfred Knopf, 1967); Duane Lockard, ed., *Governing the States and Localities* (Toronto: Macmillan, 1969); Charles Adrian, *State and Local Governments* (New York: McGraw-Hill, 1960).

26. Herbert Jacob and Michael Lipsky, "Outposts, Structure and Power: An Assessment of Changes in the Study of State and Local Politics," *Journal of Politics* 30 (1968): 514–17.

27. James W. Clarke, "Environment, Process, and Policy: A Reconsideration," *American Political Science Review* 63 (1969): 1181–82; Brian Fry and Richard Winters, "The Politics of Redistribution," *American Political Science Review* 67 (1970): 508–22.

28. The discussion of these variables is based largely on Anthony King, "Ideas, Institutions and the Policies of Governments: A Comparative Analysis: Part III," *British Journal of Political Science* 3, pt. 3 (October 1973): 409–23.

29. C. Wright Mills, *The Power Elite* (New York: Oxford University Press, 1956); and G. William Domhoff, *Who Rules America?* (Englewood Cliffs, N.J.: Prentice-Hall, 1967). For a comparable work on Western countries, see Ralph Miliband, *The State in Capitalist Society* (London: Weidenfeld and Nicholson, 1969).

30. See David Butler and Donald Stokes, *Political Change in Britain* (London: Macmillan, 1960); R. B. McCallum and Alison Readman, *The British General Election of 1945* (London: Oxford University Press, 1947); and T. O. Lloyd, *Empire to Welfare State: English History 1906–1967* (London: Oxford University Press, 1970).

31. V. O. Key, Jr., *Public Opinion and American Democracy* (New York: Alfred A. Knopf, 1961); and Michael E. Schiltz, *Public Attitudes toward Social Security, 1935–1965* (Washington, D.C.: U.S. Department of Health, Education and Welfare, 1970).

32. Henry Aaron, "Social Security: International Comparisons," in Otto Eckstein, ed., *Studies in the Economics of Income Maintenance* (Washington, D.C.: Brookings Institution, 1967), pp. 15–17.

33. Koji Taira and Peter Kilby, "Differences in Social Security Development in Selected Countries," *International Social Security Review* 22 (1969): 139–53.

34. Quoted in Philip Perlmutter, *Ethnic Education: Can It Be Relevant?* (Washington, D.C.: National Project on Ethnic America, 1974), p. 1.

35. Ibid.

36. Rowland T. Berthoff, *An Unsettled People* (New York: Harper and Row, 1971), pp. 438, 440; see also Richard M. Merelman, "Public Education and Social Structure: Three Modes of Adjustment," *Journal of Politics* 35 (1973): 789–829.

Louis Smith Is a
Man of Many Talents

FRANCIS S. HUTCHINS

When Louis Smith became dean of the Upper Division of Berea College in 1944 and dean of the College in 1947, the institution acquired an unusually valuable administrator. For several years there had been discussion and anxiety about organization. Berea, made up of three schools, experimented with a two-year Upper Division (last two years of college) and a four-year Lower Division. Fine educational theories supported such a division, but the plan did not work out as anticipated. Studies were made, a return to the unified four-year college was desired, and the change was effected. Louis Smith was welcomed as the new dean of the four-year college. He was a happy choice, prepared by turn of mind, by training, and by experience for the new responsibility.

Louis Smith was born in Fayetteville, Tennessee, in 1905. He began his educational career in Fayetteville, where he graduated from Central High School in 1923. After studying three years at Bryson College, he transferred to George Peabody College, receiving his B.S. degree in American history in 1927. He spent the next two years on the faculty of the Foundation Junior High School of Berea College, where he taught social science. A year of teaching mathematics in Harriman, Tennessee, followed, and in 1931 he was instructor in mathematics and social sciences in the Foundation School of Berea. In 1933 the Academy (last two years of high school) claimed him for the teaching of social sciences. In 1937 his name appeared in the faculty of the Lower Division of the College and in 1944 in the Upper Division as dean. His Berea years had taken him through each of the existing units of Berea College. Thus, when he became dean of the College, Louis Smith had had experience in Berea which enabled him to understand thoroughly the whole structure of the institution, its purposes, and its standards.

As a scholar Louis Smith has done important work. His thesis for the Ph.D. from the University of Chicago was "American Democracy and Military Power" (1951). It has been translated into four languages. His report "Rural Institutes of India" continues to be useful in the Far East. As a teacher in the classroom he has explicated knotty problems of politics and government. He has guided and encouraged many students through the years. A goodly number of them have entered graduate study in public administration and found significant and useful employment in state governments.

Berea College is particularly proud that Louis Smith has had the opportunity to participate in international educational thinking and planning overseas. He took with him his warm interest in people wherever he went. Members of the Commission on Rural Education in Arab lands held him in high esteem. As the group went around the world, they came to know him well. The United States became, in the minds of his Arab co-workers, a nation of friendly and concerned people because they felt these characteristics in Louis Smith.

In 1954 Dean Smith accepted an assignment for the State Department to lecture in India. It is hard to think of a more suitable representative. All his talents were called upon in his task of advising the Rural Institutes of India. Later, when the Indian teachers came for their experience in this country, Louis Smith's deftness in human relations helped to make their visit happy and profitable.

Perhaps most important of all, Louis Smith has been a treasured colleague. He was equipped with a mind that worked fast and that had a knack for spotting essential central issues and lifting them from confusing complexity. He served Berea College devotedly and tirelessly. He had the affectionate regard of his faculty and the confidence and respect of three presidents of Berea. His common and uncommon sense, his courtesy, his charm, and his delightful humor comforted all within reach—students and teachers alike. No person—student or faculty member or administrator—ever hesitated or feared to consider with him any problem, personal or collegiate.

With the retirement of Louis Smith there is hope that he will continue with vigor in his chosen field of scholarship. His colleagues hope too that his wonderful companionship may continue to warm and cheer them in the years ahead.

Bibliography of the Published
Works of Louis Smith

CAROL GESNER

"Alexis de Tocqueville and Public Administration." *Public Administration Review* 2, no. 3 (Summer 1942).

American Democracy and Military Power. Chicago: University of Chicago Press, 1951.

Translated as:

Gunji-yoku do Minshu-shugi. Translated by Sagami Takehiro. Tokyo: Hosei University Press, 1954.

Militar- und Zivilgewalt in Amerika. Translated by Helmut Bohn. Cologne: Markus Verlag, 1954.

Minjoo-jooei wa Kunsa-ryuk. Translated by Suh, Suk-soon. Seoul: Bangmoon, 1955.

La Democracia y el Poder Militar. Translated by Fernando Demarco. Buenos Aires: Editorial Bibliográfica Argentina, 1957.

"Books or People?" *Rural Higher Education* 5, no. 2, n.d.

"A Comprehensive, Calm, and Constructive Book on Accreditation in Teacher Education." *Journal of Teacher Education* 16, no. 3 (September 1965).

"The Concept of Planned Development." *Rural Higher Education* 1, no. 2 (April 1962).

"In Earnest of a Promised Contribution." In *Commemoration Volume Presented to Dr. K. G. Saiyidain*. New Delhi: Sponsoring Committee Publication, 1964.

"External Testing in Teacher Education." In *Strength through Reappraisal*. Washington, D.C.: American Association of Colleges of Teacher Education, 1963.

"The Garrison State." *Nation*, December 5, 1953.

"Improving the Quality of Higher Education in Outer Space." *Bulletin of the Bureau of School Service* 31, no. 3 (March 1959).

"The Joint Responsibility of the College and High School for General Education." *Bulletin of the Bureau of School Service* 21, no. 1 (September 1948).

"A New View of Aaron Burr." *Psychoanalytic Quarterly* 12, no. 1 (January 1943).

The Rural Institutes of Higher Education. New Delhi: Ministry of Education, Government of India, 1958.

"Switzerland and the Tensions of Europe." *South Atlantic Quarterly* 38, no. 3 (July 1939).

Contributors

NACK YOUNG AN is chairman of the Department of Political Science at Georgia State University.

THOMAS D. CLARK is Distinguished Professor of History at Eastern Kentucky University.

CAROL GESNER is professor of English at Berea College.

NORMAN L. HILL, who died in 1976, was professor of history at the University of Nebraska.

FRANCIS S. HUTCHINS is president emeritus of Berea College.

WALTER G. MUELDER is dean emeritus of the Boston University School of Theology.

D. B. ROBERTSON is professor of religion at Syracuse University.

GLEN STASSEN is professor of Christian ethics at Southern Baptist Theological Seminary.

GARY W. SYKES is associate professor of political science at Berea College.